The Pulse of the Countryside

The **Pulse**
of the
Countryside

A
**Country Doctor
Remembers**

David Webster (signature)

David Webster

The Pulse of the Countryside: A Country Doctor Remembers
David Webster

Published by Aspect Design, 2016

Designed, printed and bound by Aspect Design
89 Newtown Road, Malvern, Worcs. WR14 1PD
United Kingdom
Tel: 01684 561567
E-mail: allan@aspect-design.net
Website: www.aspect-design.net

A copy of this book has been deposited
with the British Library Board

Cover design by Katherine Wells

ISBN 978-1-908832-95-5

A BUSH DOCTOR REINVENTED

I could feel the hot sun on my face, burning, sapping every ounce of energy. The brittle brown grass—or such of it as had survived the predations of the hungry sheep—pricked my back. I shifted my position to get more comfortable. The dust around me was littered with hard, dry pellets—the droppings of the desperately foraging sheep. The acrid smell of the droppings rose in the hot air and mingled with the eddies of dust, stirred up by languid gusts of wind. Even the flies seemed to be feeling the heat as they made occasional half-hearted forays in search of beads of sweat.

As I dozed my mind went to the famine. Although drought and famine were a part of life, this was the worst famine for many years. The red volcanic earth was littered with the carcasses of sheep and cows, and even of camels. And when the animals die the old folk and the children soon follow, because their lives depend on the cattle. So death stalked the land. Images of stick-thin children, of sunken eyes that have lost all their sparkle and hope, filled my mind. Images of a wailing mother, clutching to her shrivelled breast her dead baby. Her cries of desolation hung in the hot air. And then images of our home— stark, simple, but perfectly adequate—where we ate basic but sufficient meals. And while we ate, faces peered in at every window, and desperate hands reached out—'Sagale na ken!'

'Give me food!' We did our best. We shared what we could. We distributed powdered milk for children. But it was a drop in the ocean of need. They were lean, hard, heart- breaking days.

My reverie was suddenly broken. 'Would you like another cup of tea? There are still some sandwiches left.' I sat up. My mind re-orientated itself. My eyes refocused in the bright sunlight. Not far behind us stretched a range of gentle hills, clothed in trees and bracken. Below was a vista of fields, dotted with hamlets, and beyond them another, far-distant, range of hills. No, we were not any longer in Marsabit, in northern Kenya. This was England. But the heat, and the dust, and the sheep droppings were real enough. We were picnicking on the slopes of these beautiful hills, and it was the summer of 1976, the hottest, driest summer on record. We had come from a drought to a drought. The only difference was that this English drought was a tamed, civilised kind of drought. Nobody was dying of hunger. Supermarket trolleys were still obscenely laden. Most taps spewed forth generous quantities of clean water. Oh yes! There were restrictions on the watering of gardens. Lawns had to be allowed to turn an unsightly brown. Car washing was banned—but dirty cars perform just as well as clean ones. There was no real hardship. In Marsabit life itself had hung on a knife-edge. Every new day presented the possibility of disaster and death. Here life continued happily, while the exceptional weather provided a fascinating topic of conversation for the supermarket queue, or the mums waiting outside school to collect their children.

We had come a long way over the past few weeks. A long way geographically—four thousand miles—from the deserts of northern Kenya to the gentle English countryside. But also a long way culturally—from nomadic desert tribes to English country folk. And a long way medically. In the short time I had been working in a rural English general practice I had not seen a single case of death from starvation. Nor of malaria, nor lion bite, nor kala-azar. Not one spear wound. In their place were heart disease, and stress. And various cancers, and chain saw injuries. 'Don't you miss it all—what you were doing out there? Don't you find medicine in this country a bit tame?' That was the question I was repeatedly asked in the coming months. And to tell the truth I did miss a lot of it—the responsibility of being the only doctor for thousands of square miles; the challenge of difficult diagnosis without all the investigative paraphernalia of the west; the awesome challenge of being both anaesthetist and surgeon, with just a naked light bulb or pressure lamp to see by. Our nine years in the bush had been stretching, exhausting, sometimes exhilarating, often terrifying, but so worthwhile.

Now a new phase of life was beginning. The educational needs of our children, and responsibility to family, had brought us back. And my answer to the question 'So, don't you miss it all?' was 'Yes and no.' In truth there was no comparison. This new life, this new world, this new kind of medicine, was so utterly different that one couldn't compare it. But one thing I knew—I was going to love general practice. In East Africa there had been inevitable barriers—language barriers, cultural barriers, experience barriers. I had spent my time trying to break through these barriers, and to relate to my patients, and to understand their needs, and to help them in ways that they could understand. To win trust in a world that has no scientific concept whatever of disease—no understanding of germs and infection; deep suspicion often of immunisations and preventive measures such as washing; a people to whom anaesthesia and surgery were nothing short of magic. A world of ancestral spirits and angry gods. Sometimes the gap, the barrier, had seemed uncrossable. Now I found myself on the same wavelength as my patients, entering into their fears and feelings, their joys and sorrows. I had the privilege of sharing in people's family life; of being party to their ups and downs, and to the most significant events of life—birth and death, the struggles of parenthood and of relationships, and the many crises of life. Patients, over the course of time, became friends. It was, indeed, a privilege, and privilege that was founded on mutual respect and trust. My part was to do the very best for my patients. Their part was to trust me to do it.

Doctoring in the East African bush had, for me, been quite a lonely experience, with no colleagues with whom to discuss difficult cases, or to turn to for advice. I had been the only doctor for an area the size of England. I often operated with the *Textbook of Practical Surgery* open beside me. Fortunately, my patients had thought it was doubly clever to be able, not only to operate, but also to read! Medical advice could only be obtained indirectly via my daily radio call to the Flying Doctor Service four hundred miles away. Now I had very competent colleagues with whom I could discuss cases over coffee, or I could call them in for a second opinion. I had access to laboratory tests, X-rays and scans. There were friendly consultants on the end of a phone. And in the practice itself was a team of brilliant, supportive staff—initially just receptionists, with a 'Triple Worker' (District Nurse, Health Visitor and Midwife combined in one person, Joy); in time these Health Authority roles were divided, and we also had practice nurses, dispensers, phlebotomists, attached social workers and physiotherapists, and a whole bevy of administrative staff. We were a mutually supportive team, with the common aspiration to be the best possible practice.

Our surgery premises were, when I joined the practice, purpose built, and quite small but adequate. There had been two rival practices in the village, each using a room in the doctor's house for consultations. When one of the practices took on an assistant doctor he had had to consult with patients in a curtained off area adjacent to the waiting room. This arrangement must have provided all sorts of fascinating information to the silent, all-ears occupants of the waiting room. The successors to these rival doctors had the wisdom and foresight to combine forces, and to work as partners in a new, purpose-built surgery. My arrival in the practice necessitated the adding on of an extension, and in time, with further growth in the practice, major extension and alterations were undertaken.

We wasted no time, following our arrival back from East Africa, to visit and see around the practice. We were taken on a tour of the 'patch'—a rural area covering about a ten-mile radius from the surgery. We twisted along narrow, winding country lanes, passing scattered farms and half-timbered cottages, until we were thoroughly disorientated. 'How will I ever find my way around here?' I thought to myself. On one particularly narrow and windy lane we came round a corner and suddenly a vista opened up before us. Wetlands stretched below, and beyond them a river valley. Another range of rolling hills marked the far horizon. 'Wow!' was our joint response. A warm brick house stood surveying the view. In the days ahead we often made our way to this spot. We would park under the massive horse chestnut trees opposite the house, and walk along the shady lane to the place where the view in the opposite direction opens up—more rolling blue hills. Many a time we peered over the hedge at the house. Its view over wide open spaces reminded us of the spaces of Africa. There was room to breathe. The distant hills resembled the Cherangani Hills where we had once lived, on the border of Kenya and Uganda. The house had character, it had land, it had outhouses, with all sorts of possibilities. This was our sort of place. We called it 'The Dream House'. But we could never afford it. A missionary allowance is just enough to live on, but not to save for a house. Anyway, it was not for sale. But then one day a 'For Sale' sign went up. For several weeks we ignored it—we knew we could not afford it, and did not want hopes to be raised and dashed. But then, eventually, on the urging of one of the practice partners, we asked to see round,

and we made an offer based on what we had managed to scrimp
and borrow and been promised—and to our utter joy our offer
was accepted. The dream had come true. We became the owners
of the house that was to become a dearly loved home, where
our children could grow up in the freedom of the countryside.
After our years in Africa I had come to a most wonderful and
highly regarded practice. We were living in our dream home. I
was doing the job I loved. The family had adjusted to their new
life, and were happy. We had joined a lively church where we
were warmly welcomed. We could indeed say, with the Psalmist
'The boundary lines have fallen for me in pleasant places; surely
I have a delightful inheritance.' (Psalm 16:6)

WHILE I'M HERE, DOC

'It's this fungus thing in my toenail, doc.'

It was a busy morning in surgery. The waiting room was packed. We had no appointments system then—it was first come, first served. A mild fungal infection of the toenail didn't seem to be a matter of huge importance, but it was bothering him. So we discussed the cause, the options for treatment, possible side-effects. And before we knew it the ten minutes was up. I wrote a prescription and began to wind up the conversation.

'See how it goes. Come back in a month and let's have another look.'

He hesitated, then, half way to the door, he came out with it.

'While I'm here doc I should tell you that I have had this bleeding . . .'

And so the real problem, the rather embarrassing problem, came out. The fear, even the possibility, of cancer, hiding behind a toenail. The ten-minute appointment went by the board, and it was back to taking another history, and doing a thorough examination.

In Africa diseases had often been well advanced, even gross, by the time I saw them. The patient had often spent time in the village trying out traditional remedies, and

making sacrifices to a supposedly angry God. I had been the
last resort. And so often, by the time I saw a disease, it could
be diagnosed at a hundred yards. The huge, sloughing tropical
ulcer on the leg. The pus-weeping, fly-ringed eye infection.
The enormous spleen of kala-azar, almost visible through
the abdominal wall. The red-tinged hair and pot belly of the
child with kwashiorkor. A diagnosis could often be made at
a glance. But, as I was discovering, things in England were
far more subtle. For a start most of the body is concealed
by clothing. But also men, especially, find it hard to talk
about personal things. And so the real story, the worrying
symptom, is sometimes not mentioned at first. Courage has
to be worked up. It was what I called the 'While I'm Here
Doctor Syndrome'.

Another difference to which I had to adjust was the
frequency of emotional issues in England—stress, anxiety,
depression, relationship problems. These need a lot of listening.
In Africa the tribe and family provided the support network.
And anyway people were often too busy surviving physically
to have time for their feelings. Now I found myself listening
to all kinds of sad stories, often from rather lonely people
who had little or no support network. The extended family
no longer existed. Neighbours were sometimes complete
strangers, living in their private worlds. They had nobody to
confide in.

The postman rang from an outlying village. He was
concerned that the curtains of the home of an elderly lady
whom I had been visiting were still drawn at eleven o'clock
in the morning. Was she all right? My surgery was already
running late, so I looked up the telephone number of the old
lady's next door neighbour.

'Could you please check and see if Mrs Young is all right?'
'Who is Mrs Young?'
'You know—your next door neighbour.'

'Is that her name? I've never met her.'

It turned out that Mrs Young had merely overslept. And so it was that neighbours who had been living within yards of one another for years met for the first time. It was a situation that would have been beyond credibility in Africa. Probably this was an unusually extreme case of unneighbourliness, but it was symptomatic of a society where people, couples, even families, live private lives. The Englishman's Castle Syndrome. With the demise, often, of the extended family, and the loss of influence of the clergy, the doctor has often become the one to go to, to pour out one's fears and troubles. To listen is a vital role of the GP, but listening takes time. And time is in short supply. And so it was that, with some patients, I became known as 'The late Dr Webster'—always tending to run late with my surgeries.

I soon came to recognise the 'While I'm Here Doctor Syndrome' and the 'Englishman's Castle Syndrome'. A third syndrome was the 'Health Expectation Syndrome'. People in Africa took illness for granted—the intermittent fever from chronic malaria, the infected sore, the intestinal parasite. These were normal, and had to be lived with. In Britain people expect to be well. A sore throat, a cold, an ache in a joint, are unacceptable. Something must be done. And so there is, compared with Africa, a low threshold for visiting the doctor, and a high expectation of some instant cure. This too was something I had to adjust to. Sometimes symptoms did seem trivial, and expectations of what I could do about them unrealistically high. But I had to remember that, behind every symptom was a story—often a worry that it might be something serious. Reassurance was an important form of medicine. Nevertheless there were times when one's tolerance was tried.

It was four o'clock in the morning, I was deeply asleep, when the persistent ringing of the bedside phone dragged me into consciousness. Those were the days when we GPs had responsibility for our patients twenty-four hours a day, seven days a week, 365 days a year. It was common, as the on-call doctor, to be woken at night.

'Is that the doctor?' a young female voice asked.

'Yes, speaking. How can I help you?' I replied.

'I've got toothache. Can you bring me some paracetamol?'

'How long have you had toothache?'

'It's a week now. It's getting worse.'

'Have you seen a dentist?'

'No, I haven't got a dentist.'

'Haven't you got any painkillers in the house?'

'No, nothing. Can you bring some paracetamol?'

'There's an all-night chemist open. Why don't you go there, and buy some?'

'I can't. My baby is asleep, and anyway I've had a few drinks. I can't drive.'

'Is there nobody else at home who could go?'

'No, I'm on my own.'

'What about your neighbours? Have you asked them?'

'My neighbours! I can't trouble them. They're asleep!'

'So was I until you rang!'

Rightly or wrongly, I didn't go on that particular occasion, but I might as well have, as I couldn't get off to sleep again. And another busy day was due to start a few hours later.

Adjusting to these new 'syndromes' took time. I had been quite used to being called out at night in East Africa—and there it always meant something serious, and possibly several hours in the operating theatre. It was never to deliver paracetamol tablets. Fortunately, I had been given wise advice before returning to England—do a year as a GP trainee (now termed a GP registrar) before becoming a partner. And this is what I did. I had an excellent teacher and role model in the practice trainer, my namesake David. He helped me, the bush doctor, to adjust to the different demands and expectations of English patients. To begin with I sat in on his surgeries, and did home visits with him. Each partner in the practice had a different style, and different skills and strengths. I was helped to discover mine. David had a devoted following of older patients, many of whom he visited on a regular monthly basis. Home visits with him were like a tour of old friends, each being helped and encouraged to maintain an independent living in their own home.

George was also a brilliant doctor, but different. His main interest was orthopaedics. He had a great capacity for work. His system for seeing patients in surgery was rather on the Heathrow principle. He 'stacked' them. Every spare room and space in the surgery contained one of his patients, undressing, or waiting to see him, or dressing again. There was one hazard—that of being forgotten! It did not often happen, but there was one occasion when, at the end of evening surgery, the premises were locked up, burglar alarm activated, and everyone went home. Fortunately, when half way home, the receptionist recalled a particular patient who had been 'stacked' in a side room.

She could not recall him ever having left the surgery. She drove rapidly back to the surgery and, sure enough, there was the patient, lying obediently on a couch in total darkness, waiting patiently for George.

'I was beginning to wonder if I had been forgotten,' he said.

The senior partner during my first year was also known as 'George', though his real names were John Stewart—so we had two 'Davids' and two 'Georges' in the practice, which could be a little confusing. George (senior) had an outstanding war record, having ended his service in the army as a lieutenant colonel in the RAMC, with a Military Cross and bar, and mention in dispatches. He was a kind, shy, modest, self-effacing man, who never spoke of his war record. He had become one of the two general practitioners in the village—two separate practices vying with one another, their patients passionately loyal to 'their' doctor. George (senior) belonged very much to the old school of GPs—no fuss, none of this modern paraphernalia, he called a spade a 'spade' and not an 'excavation implement'. We had a small dispensary, with shelves of bottles and boxes of medicine. There was no dispenser or pharmacist—at the end of each consultation we went to the dispensary ourselves to dispense whatever we had prescribed. For George this was a welcome opportunity for a quick smoke, and we would often find him leaning on the counter, cigarette in hand, enjoying a brief respite. On the dispensary shelf stood two bottles of George's special medicine. One was a bottle of green liquid, and the other was red. I never did discover exactly what they contained—possibly a few vitamins, but little else, except colouring. George used these for more nebulous illnesses—neurasthenia, general debility, etc. If one colour didn't work he might try the other. Without a controlled trial it was impossible to know whether they had any effect at all, other than placebo, but his patients seemed happy with them, and came back for more.

Half way through my trainee year George (senior) decided to go part-time, and then retire. The partners invited me to join them, as a Principal Partner, and so it was, in due course, that my brass plate joined theirs. The receptionists covered it with a paper hand towel held by Sellotape, and we had an unveiling ceremony. A bottle of champagne was opened. It was indeed a proud day. I had come to work with wonderful colleagues among, for by far the most part, lovely patients, many of whom were to become my friends over the next thirty years.

It was the tradition in the practice that each partner had a medical commitment outside the practice. It kept us fresh, and gave us a wider horizon. David had a particular interest in diabetes, and did sessions in the diabetic clinic at the district hospital. George's interest being in orthopaedics he did sessions in the nearest Accident and Emergency department. He was also a medical politician, and served for many years on local and district medical committees. I took on the role of school doctor to twelve local village primary schools, and to two secondary schools, as well as being responsible for local child health clinics. Doing repetitive health checks on babies and on school entry children could have become boring. And yet it never was, because each child was different. Even babies have their own personalities. And because one was looking out for any problem, whether of vision, hearing, speech, mobility, or whatever, in order that it could be dealt with early, one could not afford to let it become boring. Bored doctors miss things. Over the years the work diminished. Sadly four of the village primary schools were closed as being financially unsustainable. Furthermore a succession of 'Hall Reports', by an eminent child health specialist, gradually reduced the amount of health screening of children. The relatively small number of problems picked up at such clinics were reckoned to be 'not cost effective'. It may not have been cost effective in general terms, but for the child who happens to have a congenital dislocation of hip, or curvature of the spine, or a vision problem, that was picked up early, it was highly cost effective.

Clinics in secondary schools focussed on children with problems that had already been identified, and which affected their schooling. Regular meetings with school staff (called Selective Conferences) ensured that their problems—perhaps muscular dystrophy, or cystic fibrosis, or colour blindness, or maybe emotional problems from bullying or a difficult home environment—were understood and provided for in the school environment. I worked closely with my colleagues, the school nurses. Immunisation days, when we did the routine jabs for tetanus and polio, or TB, were guaranteed to cause a stir of excitement and fear among the pupils. We devised methods of reducing the spread of panic—a fast flow helps, with short queuing time, which is when the hysteria builds up. 'Did it hurt? Did it hurt? Oh no! I'm scared!' sort of talk. For the tetanus injection and polio drops we had an excellent system. The polio drops are bitter, so the school nurse would administer those (without the luxury of a sugar lump), and while the pupil was busy protesting at the taste, and proclaiming 'Yuk!' I would slip the tetanus injection into their arm without them even noticing it. 'Is that it? Have you done it?' they would often say in surprise and relief.

I was always impressed by the high standards of care and understanding shown by school staff. On one occasion, at a large secondary school to which I was school doctor, the school nurse and I were having a Selective Conference with the Deputy Head. Our meeting was interrupted from time to time by a knock on her office door, and a boy or girl would slip her an envelope and go. It was intriguing.

'What are all these notes?' I asked.

'February fourteenth. Valentines Day!' she explained. 'My job is to distribute their lovelorn messages to the ones they secretly admire.'

'Good on you!' I thought. I was impressed that a very busy deputy head had the time and care to take an interest in the children's emotional lives. It no doubt also helped her to keep tabs on the erratic beatings of her pupils' heartstrings. Even more than her care for them, I was impressed by the pupils' trust in her, to deliver their Valentine messages to the right recipients. Trust is such a vital ingredient in both the pupil/teacher relationship, and also in the patient/doctor relationship. 'Trust me, I'm a doctor' should be more than an axiom; certainly more than a joke—the caption to the picture of a crocodile. It should be a reality.

COUNTRY FOLK AND COUNTY FOLK

We hadn't been here long when we had an unexpected addition to the family. It all began with a phone call in the middle of surgery. Mr Orland had had a fall, and had cut his head. David (my Trainer) and I had been visiting his wife until her recent death, and we had been concerned as to how Mr Orland would cope. He was becoming rather confused, and the bereavement had hit him hard. He and his wife had lived in their little cottage for all their married lives. She had been the organiser, the coper, the rock of their marriage. And now she was gone.

I grabbed a suture kit and my medical case and drove to the cottage. The scene that greeted me was one of carnage and total chaos. Mr Orland was sitting at a table in the centre of the living room, pressing a blood-soaked towel to his head. There was blood everywhere. The room was reminiscent of Tracey Emin's famous bed, but with the addition of a recent murder—a picture of complete disorder and mess. Mr Orland had been trying to mend a lamp, and bare, live electric wires protruded from the flex. Meanwhile a small, fluffy, black puppy, that resembled a hyperactive hearthrug, was rushing round the room in a state of great excitement. As I cleaned Mr Orland's head, and found the laceration, and began to suture it, I was distracted by the antics of the puppy.

'Where has she come from?' I asked.

'The social worker thought I needed a companion,' he said.
'She brought it,'

'Is the puppy helping?' I asked, surveying the scene. Around
the room were randomly placed dishes of Mr Orland's food,
gone cold, and dishes of dog food. I wondered who was eating
what. It was also clear that Mr Orland's fall had been caused by
the puppy, whose manic racing round the room bore no regard
for human feet.

'Take it away! Please take it away!' pleaded Mr Orland.

I pondered as I stitched. What was I to do? Should I ring
the social worker, and ask her to remove the puppy? But that
could take a while to organise, and meanwhile Mr Orland was
at serious risk of another fall. Should I take the puppy away
with me? What would Rosemary think if I arrived home with
a very lively puppy? We had had a little dog in East Africa, but
had vowed not to get another until we were well settled.

Another deterrent factor became clear. As I stitched Mr
Orland's head I became increasingly conscious of an ammonia-
like smell in the room. Dog wee! I had better enquire.

'Do you have any problem from the puppy making puddles?'
I asked.

Mr Orland thought a while.

'No! No problem at all' he said. I sniffed the air again. The
smell was even stronger. Silence. Then Mr Orland added, 'They
all soak into the carpet you see.'

Manic puppy or not, mess or no mess, puddles or no puddles,
the fact was that I could not leave that puppy and Mr Orland
in the same room. And so it was that our family increased that
day. I arrived home with a fluffy black bundle in my arms—a
black bundle that in no time found her way into the hearts
of our family. We gave her the same name as our much loved
little dog in Africa—'Chepta', meaning 'Little girl' in the Pokot
language. She and our children grew up together, until finally
at a ripe old age, we buried her under the lilac tree.

For poor old Mr Orland it was not such a happy end. A month later he accidentally set his house on fire. Taken into care, in a rest home, he kept escaping, and trying to find his way back home. On one occasion, he actually turned up in a taxi at his old home, with all its memories. His dementia worsened, and he gradually faded from this life. For us, his memory lived on in the lovely, lively Chepta.

As I had stood stitching Mr Orland's head that day I noticed—apart from the mess and the odour—photographs around the room—photographs of former days, good days, when he had been young and vigorous and able and in love. Photographs of their wedding day. Photographs of him in uniform in the war. It reminded me never just to see people as they are, but also as they have been. To see all the potential and the gifts, all the stories and past achievements, that are perhaps now obscured by age or illness or dementia. In years to come, when I was doctor to a nursing home, with a busy dementia unit, we had a rule that, whenever possible, we displayed in each person's bedroom photographs of them in days gone by. It was a reminder to staff and visitors that the frail, confused, incontinent person before them was still the same person that they used to be.

To step into some of the country cottages in our practice 'patch' was to step back into another century. Some cottages had never been modernised—no electricity, no running water, no central heating, a stone sink in the kitchen. But what you have never had you don't miss. The Fulchers cottage was like that, and they were the perfect pair to live in it, plucked out of the Dickensian era. A tiny half-timbered cottage, it had one room downstairs, one up, a tiny kitchen and bathroom, and an outdoor latrine down the garden path. A warm, welcoming coal fire burned constantly in the grate, summer and winter, and this is what they cooked on. There was forever a blackened kettle simmering on the coals. The centre of the room was filled with a sturdy wooden table covered in clean, carefully arranged newspaper. An old-fashioned oak sideboard, covered with knick-knacks, was the only other furnishing, apart from the two armchairs, on either side of the hearth, on which Mr and Mrs Fulcher sat. And there, in those chairs, is where this tiny Darby and Joan couple seemed to spend their lives—Mrs Fulcher knitting endless pairs of socks, Mr Fulcher studying the newspaper before consigning it to its role as the next table cloth. They were always excessively polite and grateful, and warmly welcoming.

I was called, on one occasion, following a rare argument, not between the Fulchers themselves, but between her and her brother. It was to do with the inheritance of a certain picture. The dispute had become a bit physical, and a pot figurine had been accidentally knocked off the sideboard. It had hit Mrs Fulcher on the chest, and so I had been called. I realised that I was there, not because of any fear of a serious injury, but to bear witness to the event, and to add a certain legitimacy to her hurt pride.

'I had better have a look at your chest, and check that there are no rib injuries,' I said.

As she began to undress I wished I had been content with a prod through her clothing. The undressing was a major and time-consuming event. I counted as the layers were unpeeled, one by one. Coat, cardigan, dress, vests, corset, flannel jacket, bodice. I could not have given a name to some of the items of clothing, but there were nine layers in all. When we finally got down to skin level there was, not surprisingly, no sign of injury. It would have taken a high velocity bullet to penetrate her protective layers. Sometime later I was very touched when, as a 'thank you', the Fulchers presented me with a small package, wrapped in newspaper. It was a small pot figurine, possibly the very one that fell on her.

The generosity of many of the country folk was touching.

I might finish my home calls with a cabbage, or half a dozen new laid eggs, or a pheasant, or even, on occasion, a dead, unskinned rabbit. Every Christmas without fail each partner was given a turkey by a farmer who had a smallholding, but was not very wealthy. Mrs Hill was another source of regular gifts. She lived alone in a remote cottage. The track to her house ('road' would be an exaggeration) needed slow and careful negotiation. She took the precaution of accepting conventional treatments for her chronic ailments, but also various potions and remedies from healers, with whom she was in touch. Her forte was home-made wine. It came in all sorts of varieties— rose hip, dandelion, elderflower, elderberry. All tasted exactly the same—very sweet and very potent. She never failed to give me a bottle of her latest brew when I made a home call. I would lay the bottle in the well of my car, and put it through the 'track test' (originally taught me by my trainer, David). If the bottle survived the journey back to the road, without seeping sticky fluid onto my car mat, it would join the collection at home. If it leaked it inevitably ended up in a certain bush at the end of the track. Anyone in search of vintage home-made wine would do well to search that bush. My home collection of Mrs Hill's wines came into their own every Christmas, when the year's collection formed the basis of a tasty and powerful punch. I was very touched one day when I met Mrs Hill's daughter, who said, 'Oh, Mother does like your visits. Each time she says "Dr Webster looked so nice today".'

I was inwardly preening myself when she added, 'You know, her eyesight is very poor these days.'

Another regular recipient of Mrs Hill's bacchanalian generosity was our local postman, Martin. Martin drove along the country lanes in his little red post office van, distributing letters and kindness. Nothing was ever too much trouble. He kept an eye on old folk. He delivered medicines from the surgery, carried in the coal for the elderly, changed the odd light bulb, always had time for a chat, and was loved by all. We were at the end of his circuitous round, so he always came in for a cup of coffee, and (hopefully) a slice of cake or a home-made biscuit. He loved it when our children were at home, and he could engage in animated discussions. Friends staying in our house when we were away were astonished to see Martin arrive with the post, go into the kitchen, make himself a cup of coffee, emerge with the garage key, get out the mower, mow the lawn—and then proceed on his way, as though this was quite normal activity for a postman. Perhaps for our children the most popular thing that Martin ever did was to bring a newborn orphan lamb that needed to be bottle-fed. It was given the name Mint Sauce by the children, and it became a household pet. Our dog Chepta would endlessly round up the lamb on the lawn until, when Mint Sauce had had enough, she would head butt Chepta, and in lamb language say 'That's enough!'

The majority of our patients were delightful—whether the old fashioned country folk, or those living in modern housing estates or council houses. The elite too, of whom we had a fair share, were kindly, appreciative people—gentlefolk, county folk, whom it was a pleasure to know and to treat. But every now and then one came across rudeness and presumption, which helped to counter any self-congratulation or complacency. I had completed my year as trainee in the practice and I had just become a partner. A new trainee was starting that day, and it was going to be my turn to take him with me on my rounds. Just as David and George had been my role models, now it was up to me to show him how good family medicine is practiced. I could prove to him the value of home visits, of seeing patients in their home context, of helping the elderly and frail to feel 'looked-after'. As was our custom we doctors met over coffee to allocate the day's visits. Miss Forbes-Fortescue had requested a home visit by her usual doctor, the senior partner. It happened to be the senior partner's half day, so that particular visit was allocated to me—together with my apprentice, the new trainee. I had never met Miss Forbes-Fortescue, and the partners did not enlighten me.

The trainee and I arrived at the rather grand house, with its long, straight, imposing gated driveway. It was clear from the start that she was a 'doggie' lady. There were two warning signs at the gate: 'Beware of the Dog' and 'Beware—Dogs Loose'. We proceeded cautiously on foot up the drive, to be met by furious barking and yapping from within, by what sounded like a whole pack of dogs. A maid met us at the door, releasing, as she opened it, an overpowering odour of dog. She looked a little surprised to see two of us, neither being the usual doctor. We were shown upstairs to the large bedroom. And there, in a huge double bed, her tall frame propped up on pillows, her coiffeur immaculate, her red lipstick luminescent, reposed Miss Forbes-Fortescue herself.

'Who the hell are you?' she demanded in an imperious voice, peering at us over her glasses as we entered her sanctuary.

I began to introduce ourselves. She did not want to know—we could have been the Kray twins as far as she was concerned.

'I asked for my doctor, not you whoever you are,' she bawled.

I explained that her doctor was not available, and she would have to make do with us, but she dissolved into a fit of coughing, drowning out my words.

I offered to examine her, but she would have none of it. This upstart and his apprentice were not going to touch her. And so, having made it clear that 'her' doctor (the one she clearly considered that she owned) would not be available until at least the next day, we left. So much for showing our new trainee the joys and rewards of home visits! It was not the last of my encounters with Miss Forbes-Fortescue over the coming years.

WHAT DID YOU SAY, DOCTOR?

I thought, when we came back from Africa, that communication difficulties were over.

There I had spoken reasonable Kiswahili, but many of my rural patients had spoken only their tribal languages—and my practice areas had covered many different tribes.

Sometimes to take a medical history involved a chain of translation. I would ask a question in English or Kiswahili. It would be translated into, say, Borana, and then another translator would translate to, say, Rendille. When the answer to my question eventually arrived back it sometimes bore no relevance whatever to the original question. I might ask, 'How long have you had the pain?' and the reply might eventually come back 'My grandmother.' It was sometimes like a game of Chinese whispers. Words, questions, often had to be accompanied by a lot of gesticulations, pointings, rubbings of the tummy, and raised, questioning eyebrows.

I was soon to discover that things were not always straightforward in England. One of the very first patients whom I saw was both stone deaf and completely blind. The only way to communicate with him was to spell out words with a finger on his palm. He felt the shape of the letters. His wife patiently and lovingly communicated with him in this way, as did anybody else. It was a slow process.

I got to know a delightful Indian couple, both professionals. Their English was fluent, and there was no communication problem with them. But things changed when her elderly and frail parents came to live with them. Neither parent spoke English. From time to time they required home visits. If the daughter was at home there was no problem—she translated into Gujarati. But if she was at work there was a problem. With many laughs and gesticulations, and the odd word of English, the old couple and I usually managed to get the gist of the matter. But it was a hit and miss process. Then the day came when I called to see them when the daughter was at home, and I happened to ask her how long it was since her parents had come to England from India.

'Four years' replied the daughter. 'But actually it was Kenya they came from. That is where they used to live.'

My ears pricked up. Kenya! I turned to the parents.

'Jambo! Habari gani? Mnasema Kiswahili?'

Their faces lit up, because, of course, they spoke Kiswahili. The communication barrier was down, and from that day we had no problem whatever communicating. It was always a pleasure to take the current trainee with me on visits to that home, and to surprise and impress them with my knowledge of what they took to be Gujarati.

'It is essential, in general practice,' I would tell the trainee, with a straight face, 'to learn to speak whatever language your patients speak.'

Misunderstandings could occur quite apart from any language barrier. A lady had been on a course of antibiotics, and returned for a check-up.

'How are you doing?' I asked.

'My cough is much better, but I'm not happy about all the weight I have put on.'

'Weight? How come? Antibiotics don't make you put on weight!'

'It was all the food I had to eat with them.'

'Food? Why?'

'The label on the antibiotics said so.'

'Really? Let's have a look.'

There it was: *Take one capsule three times daily with food. Complete course.*

'You see, it was having to have a complete course each time—cooked breakfasts, lunches and suppers. I never normally eat that much.'

For future occasions I pointed out the meaning and importance of completing a course of tablets, not of food.

It was midnight when Mr Foster rang. He sounded rather confused.

'Can you come and sort me out, doc?'

Mr Foster lived on his own in an old house down a winding lane not far from us. I put clothes on over my pyjamas and set off. A tawny owl was calling from the nearby ash woods. I slowed down for a badger, which bustled busily along the lane in front of the car before peeling off into the hedgerow. On night calls you never knew what you might come across next—night jars sitting in the road; foxes; suicidal rabbits in abundance. The old brick house was in total darkness when I arrived. Stupidly I had forgotten my torch. I took out the penlight torch that I used for examining throats, and searched by its pen-sized beam for the door latch. The door was unlocked.

'Hello!' I called. A muffled reply came from somewhere upstairs. I groped my way up a steep staircase.

'Where are you?' I called, as though engaged in a fun game of hide-and-seek. Again a muffled reply from a bedroom. By the light of my torch I could just make out a form in a large double bed.

'Reach above the bed, doc. There's a gas light. Pull the string down and it will light.'

It did, and its glow revealed a rather sick looking Mr Foster.

His face appeared to be slightly lop-sided. Was it the shadow of the gas lamp or had he had a stroke? I proceeded to check him over, including a neurological examination. This involves testing each of the twelve cranial nerves, and the examination follows a well-tried protocol.

'Follow my finger with your eyes—side to side; up and down. Look at my light, now look away. Screw your eyes up tight. Frown. Turn your head to the right; now to the left. Pop out your tongue. Show me your teeth . . .'

At this point Mr Foster seemed to have become weary of the examination; or perhaps he had a sudden need to visit the toilet. Instead of drawing back his lips as requested he slowly swung his legs over the side of the bed, and struggled to sit up. I helped him to his feet.

'Where do you need to go?' I asked.

'Over here', he replied, heading with unsteady steps for the huge chest of drawers.

'Here they are!' he said. And there, reposing in a glass of water, was a magnificent pair of false teeth! On future occasions I clarified the expression used for testing the seventh cranial nerve.

'Pull back your lips,' I would say. Not 'Show me your teeth.'

Communication can break down for all sorts of reasons—deafness; language barriers; regional accents; mishearing; misunderstanding; a speech defect; muttering. I have been surprised by the number of times when patients have said to me things such as (in exaggerated form):

'I'll never forget that advice you gave me doctor—always to swallow tablets while standing on one leg with a daffodil in my ear'.

And I would think to myself:

'When did I ever say that? I would never have said that!'

And the patient would continue:

'Brilliant advice! I am so grateful. You were so right. I'll never forget that. I've passed the advice on to friends.'

And I would smile, and shrug my shoulders modestly, as though to say 'Well it was the least I could do', and wonder how on earth that misunderstanding arose.

Some communications can be unexpected. I was examining a young mother's abdomen in antenatal clinic. Her three-year-old was sitting in my chair, watching. The time came to listen to the baby's heart with the sonicaid.

'Let's see if we can hear the baby,' I said to the little girl, as I applied the sonicaid over the uterus. At that moment a message for me from the receptionist came over the intercom. The voice said: 'Dr Webster, would you ring me when you are free?'

The little girl gave a shriek of delight, leapt off my chair, and ran round the room shouting 'I heard the baby! I heard the baby! It spoke!' Nothing would convince her otherwise, and why should it?

QUO VADIS?

A question that every GP must ask his or her patients nowadays is 'Quo vadis?' 'Where are you going?' Or perhaps more often the question should be 'Where have you been?' We live in a shrinking world. Students travel. Gap year students spend time abroad, experiencing other cultures, and widening their horizons. Older folk travel too, not only to the usual tourist hotspots, but sometimes to the remotest parts of the world. It has all become possible due to the burgeoning air industry, and relatively cheap flights; and also to increased spending power in the west. A week in Blackpool is no longer an attractive option for many middle class folk. Better a week in the Maasai Mara, or exploring the Amazon. Of course, there is a consequence. Not only do travellers come back laden with exotic mementos, but also, sometimes, with exotic germs. Every year people die in Britain because they forget to tell their doctor, and he or she forgets to ask, where they have been.

Probably the greatest risk is malaria, particularly the Falciparum brand of African malaria, which can spread to the brain, as cerebral malaria, and kill within hours. The early symptoms can easily be mistaken for flu. 'Take some paracetamol and go to bed, and see how you are tomorrow,' says the doctor who has not asked 'Where have you been?'

There may be no tomorrow. But malaria is far from being the only tropical disease seen nowadays in general practice.

From time to time I was delighted to recognise old friends—such as the tumbu fly. A patient came to see me with a boil on her thigh. They were recently back from a holiday in East Africa. The boil had started while on holiday, and had got steadily worse, not responding to hot soaks or antiseptic cream.

I looked closely with a magnifying glass. Never had the patient had such close interest shown in a mere boil. And I gave a (modest) whoop of delight. There, in the centre of the boil, was a small pit, and in the depths of the pit I could just see the wriggling rear end of a large maggot. It was indeed a tumbu fly. This tropical fly loves to lay its eggs on damp clothing, such as that hanging on a washing line.

When the clothes are next worn, and especially if they have not been ironed, a small grub hatches from the egg and burrows into the adjacent skin. There it grows, producing a painful abscess. If left undisturbed it will eventually pupate, and finally hatch into an adult fly. This patient had hung her smalls out to dry, while on safari in Kenya. Her particular tumbu fly was destined to have its life cycle cut short. I pressed gently on the sides of the boil, and, just as the discomfort for the patient was becoming too much, out popped a large, wriggling maggot. Job done! The maggot can be killed by smothering the boil with Vaseline, but this leaves a dead maggot *in situ*, which has to be absorbed by the body, so prolonging the agony.

Jigger fleas were another delight, which presented at surgery on two occasions. The jigger flea lives in dusty soil in tropical countries. Having mated it waits for a passing victim. It burrows into the toe, usually alongside the toenail, causing intense itching in the process. It lays a sac of eggs, which develop into baby jigger fleas, which eventually burst out, leaving a hole in the toe which is very susceptible to infection. During my barefoot childhood in Kenya each day ended with the jigger ceremony, when our toes were inspected, and any culprits were extracted with a safety pin that had been sterilised on the pressure lamp. The greatest achievement in the jigger-removing stakes was to extract a complete sac of jigger plus eggs, without bursting it. One that I saw in the surgery had reached this stage, and provided me with some satisfying and nostalgic moments, not entirely appreciated by the patient.

Sleeping sickness, or trypanosomiasis, was always a possibility for anyone who had visited a game park in Central or East Africa. The trypanosome is carried by the tsetse fly, which hangs out in shady trees in the African savannah, flying out on forays to bite and suck blood from wild animals or cattle, and so infecting them. Humans are incidental victims. In the past large swathes of Africa have been rendered uninhabitable due to tsetse flies. I never saw—or perhaps more truthful to tell—I never diagnosed, a case. I saw plenty of sleepy patients, but sleepy for other reasons. Our young daughter, however, was taught about sleeping sickness at school, and I was asked to contribute to the lesson. My poetic powers reached their zenith with the following poem:

> There once was a soft-hearted tsetse,
> Who liked to be called Betsy, spelled Bsetse.
> She sat in the shade,
> And rather than raid
> To suck blood, she sipped Coke, or a Psepse.

We had one case of tick typhus, and several people suspected of having bilharzia (schistosomiasis), caught by swimming in tropical lakes or rivers. Perhaps the most unexpected exotic diagnosis was a tiger bite—sustained by a child who, perhaps unwisely, stroked a 'tame' tiger at a nearby wildlife park. We partners did a tropical diseases presentation, 'Exotica Tropicalis', to our fellow GPs at a clinical meeting. Our partner, David, spoke about the local cholera epidemic of 1830 ('Being the senior partner', he said 'I am the only one who can remember it.'). We each then presented cases of tropical diseases that we had seen.

Perhaps the most memorable case was that of Jim. He had been working for some time in West Africa, and had recently returned to Britain. Two days before Christmas he developed flu-like symptoms. He knew, and I knew, that we could not write it off as flu. He had taken his anti-malarial tablets regularly, but cases of resistance to the normal prophylactics were occurring. I took blood tests, including the 'thick films' needed to check for malaria. The result came back: 'No malaria parasites seen'. By then Jim was feeling somewhat better. Perhaps it was flu after all. Christmas Day dawned, and Jim's temperature had soared again. He felt very ill. The partner on duty on Christmas Day was George. He examined Jim in the surgery, but found no specific symptoms or signs—just a very high temperature, and feeling like death. George was faced with a quandary. Here was a man recently returned from West Africa, with a high fever, and a negative blood test for malaria. Could it be Lassa fever, or Marburg or Ebola—all very serious viral diseases, known to exist in West Africa? George rang the specialist in Tropical Diseases in Birmingham for advice, and the advice was 'Yes, it could be some deadly virus.' George was now a contact, and at potential risk himself. The consultant told him that he and Jim should remain isolated in the surgery, and he would come immediately from Birmingham to assess the situation.

George and Jim celebrated their Christmas lunch together in the surgery—though in Jim's case he didn't feel like too much celebration. George's wife passed them Christmas lunch through the surgery window. Eventually the tropical disease consultant arrived. He donned protective clothing and mask, and entered the surgery looking rather like a spaceman. There was nothing specific to find—Jim would have to go to Birmingham, into isolation, as a suspected case of Lassa Fever.

An ambulance could not be used, as potential contamination would have put it out of use. So Jim was driven to Birmingham in the consultant's car. The residents of Birmingham might have been surprised to see a sick looking passenger being driven by a fully masked and gowned spaceman.

Test results during the next day or two ruled out Lassa Fever, or any of the other possible tropical viral diseases. The diagnosis was made of 'a small patch of pneumonia'. We greeted this diagnosis with some scepticism—'small patches of pneumonia' do not make people as ill as Jim had been. However he was discharged home, on antibiotics, and there was no doubt that he looked better.

Better, that is, until New Year's Day, when it was my turn to be on call. Jim rang.

'My temperature's right up again, Doctor.'

This would fit the cycle of malaria. It so happened that the Pathologist on call that day had spent some years working in West Africa, and he lived in our practice area. 'Take another thick film and bring it round to my house' he said. Together, in his kitchen, we stained the slide, and examined it under a microscope that he had at home. It was swarming with malaria parasites. We had caught the blood sample at the right phase of the parasite's cycle. Jim was admitted to the local hospital, and treated with quinine, and in no time was on the mend. Malaria is a notifiable disease, and when I came to fill in the report, and it asked 'How and where was this disease diagnosed?' it gave me great pleasure to say 'By thick film in the pathologist's kitchen in the village'.

Global warming will increase the risks of tropical diseases reaching, or even becoming endemic on, our shores. Doctors will increasingly need to have a high suspicion index for diseases that at one time were hardly ever seen in this country. It doesn't take a moment to ask 'Have you by any chance been abroad?' but that moment could save a life.

FROM BIRTH

The joy and privilege of family medicine is that you see life from beginning to end. You are sometimes there at the breathtaking moment when a baby arrives, and you see that baby grow and develop, into a toddler, a school child, a challenging teenager, and maybe an adult. So much of medicine is inevitably to do with sickness; with dealing with people who are in a place where they have no wish to be. But pregnancy and birth is something else. It is, usually, wanted and welcomed, and brings anticipation and sheer joy.

The midwives and we GPs worked as a team. We shared the care of 'our mums'. Antenatal clinics were positive, happy times. From time to time we had home deliveries, which were usually celebratory times—nerve-wracking sometimes, until the baby was safely delivered, but then occasions for tears of joy. A birth in the family is a life-changing, breath-holding moment. The world stands still in awe. It is a moment imprinted for ever on the memory. And we, as GPs, have the profound privilege sometimes of sharing that miraculous moment. When all the sweating and groaning and gasping is over (the mother's as well as the father's) dad produces the bottle of champagne that has been put aside for this moment, and family, midwife and doctor, drink a toast together to the health and happy future of this new little being. For me the icing on the cake was to be asked, occasionally, to say a prayer of thanks and blessing for this new life.

The couple who presented themselves in surgery one day were, to say the least, unconventional. They sported tattoos and piercings in abundance, and eye-catching hairstyles. But it was not their appearance that struck me most—it was their demeanour. They seemed on edge, suspicious, almost hostile. I wondered, was my body language conveying to them the wrong message? I hoped not. It was not my place to judge anyone on their appearance.

'What can I do for you?' I asked the inevitable question.

'It's like this you see. We're expecting a baby. And we want it to be a natural birth—no messing about or interfering by you people. And we are going to have it at home, our way. We're just telling you because we've been told we've got to.'

There was a note of challenge in his voice, almost daring me to disagree with him.

'That's great news!' I said. 'So let's talk about it.'

It was to be her first baby. I took a medical history, and she let me examine her, with husband hovering protectively behind my shoulder, lest I inflict on her some medical outrage. I explained the normal procedure in pregnancy and delivery, and why, and the importance of involving a midwife in her care. I explained that, for a home delivery, we would expect a certain standard of facilities. I could see their eyes beginning to glaze over at this point. I explained that the midwife would want to visit their home, and that I too would like to make a home visit, not least so that I would know exactly where they lived when the day of delivery came. Having said all this, I promised that, in so far as it was safe, we would let them do things 'their way'. They went out somewhat happier and less hostile than when they came in.

The day came for my home visit. Pauline, the midwife, had already been, and her travel directions and home report had been rather worrying.

'Turn off the lane opposite a cottage full of dogs; drive for half a mile along a rutted track to a rather derelict farm; then bear right up a hill. You'll see some old buses at the top of the hill. Just head for them. There is no road.'

The 'cottage full of dogs' was unmistakable—at every mud-smeared window faces of barking dogs peered out. The cottage was one big kennel, with the owner living in one room upstairs. I turned onto the track. It had been raining and the ruts contained some deep puddles. But it was when I came to the hill after the derelict farm that my journey came to a sticky end. The wheels of the car spun in the glutinous mud, and I abandoned it to walk the last bit. As I neared the collection of old buses and caravans, my shoes heavy with clods, I was greeted by a cacophony of barking, as a bevy of nondescript dogs appeared from every direction. Were they a welcoming party or an assassination squad? One dog, I noted, had just three legs, but that deficiency was made up for by its bark.

The dogs reluctantly let me by, and I knocked on the door of the nearest bus. I was redirected to another, larger single-decker bus, and stepped into a different, alternative world. A double bed dominated the room, and a beautiful wooden armchair, carved from a gnarled tree trunk, sat next to it. There was a bookcase fixed to the wall, with a few well-thumbed books, and a small camping gas cooker. A paraffin lamp hung from the roof. The heavy aroma of incense wafted from a burning joss stick. Three things were noticeably and worryingly absent—any sign of electricity, any sign of running water, and any sign of a telephone line! This was clearly not an ideal place for a home delivery. We came to a sort of agreement—that the midwife and I would go along with a home delivery, provided that, if anything were to go wrong, they would agree to a transfer to hospital. As we negotiated our deal I had visions of someone having to run down to the farm to make a telephone call (in those days before the advent of mobile phones), and then of an ambulance trying to make its way up that slippery slope to the buses. One hoped that any emergency would not be too urgent an emergency. But there was little option. This couple, come what may, were going to have a home delivery, and we could wash our hands of them, or negotiate a compromise. Better a compromise.

It was at a weekend when Pauline, the midwife, rang from the farm to say that our hippy friend was in early labour. Pauline also had another lady in labour, so would I go and sit in at the bus while she tended to her other patient? There had been no rain, and I was able to drive up to the buses. A wonderfully unconventional domestic scene awaited me. Our patient in labour was lying on a piece of carpet, laid out on the dusty ground outside the bus. Her husband was hovering, uncertain how to be useful. He produced a camp chair for me. The three-legged dog lay next to the patient. Every now and then it scrambled to its feet, and made a lopsided circuit of the carpet, before lying down again. A chicken scratched in the dust next to us, unearthing bits of rubbish, including the odd hypodermic needle. As our friend's labour pains grew stronger, and her groans louder, the chicken gave her quizzical looks, as though to say 'Why all the fuss? I just pop them out.'

Two hours passed. I couldn't leave. I couldn't communicate with Pauline or with home. The sun began to sink behind the hills, and there was a chill in the air. It was decided to move inside the bus. At this point Pauline arrived, and I retired to the tree trunk armchair. While Pauline busied herself with an examination to assess progress, I surveyed the books on the bookshelf above the bed. The titles were all of a kind: *Natural Childbirth*, *Birth Without Medical Interference*, *Hypnobirthing*, *Natural Remedies for Pregnancy*, *Reclaim Your Body*, *Holistic Childbirth* and so on. The very titles seemed to be conveying a clear message to me—'sit in your tree chair and keep out of this.' As the bus grew darker the paraffin lamp was lit. The smell of paraffin combined with that of the joss stick to create a cosy, sleepy atmosphere. I could have been back in Africa. Everything glided to a climax, and with a triumphant final shout another little hippy slid into the world. The usual injection of syntometrine had been refused, but, to Pauline's and my relief, the placenta delivered, and, after an appropriate interval, the proud new dad performed the cord-cutting ceremony. He reverently took away the placenta, and we did not ask what he would do with it—frying pan and onions crossed our minds. The baby was immediately put to the breast, and the three-legged dog wandered over to look at her, and possibly to check the number of legs she had. No doubt, outside, the hen settled on its perch with relief that the prolonged and painful egg-laying ceremony was at last over. And Pauline and I drove back down the hill and into the real world, with the grateful thanks of our friends echoing in our ears. It was the beginning of a strong and positive relationship with that alternative and often suspicious community, in their buses and caravans on the hill.

Over the years, I saw many babies arrive in the world. I sometimes see those babies now, with their own babies. The arrival of one particular baby went down in the annals of the surgery. Rita had come for a routine antenatal check. She had only a few days to go until the baby was due. As I examined her I was conscious of very definite tightenings of the womb.

'Are you getting any pain with these contractions?' I asked.

'Well yes! They are a bit sore,' Rita replied.

'I think you are in early labour,' I said, with profound insight. 'I think we had better ring your husband at work and get him to come and pick you up, and collect your case from home and take you in to the maternity unit.'

I rang Martin, and he said he would be with us in about half an hour. Meanwhile it was obvious that Rita's contractions had strengthened. We examined her, and found labour to be progressing quite fast.

'I don't think this baby is going to wait for Martin,' I said. 'We had better call an ambulance to take you straight to hospital.'

The ambulance came very quickly, blue lights and siren and all. But by this time Rita was beginning to want to push.

'This baby is waiting for nobody,' I said, as we transferred Rita to the treatment room. By now Martin had arrived. The midwife, Pauline, was already present and the district nurse. The room was filling up.

Then one of the ambulance men took me aside and said, 'I have never seen a baby born. Would she mind if I watched?'

Would she mind?

'Not at all' said Rita between her pantings and pushings. 'The more the merrier! Everyone's welcome!'

She was, by now, beyond caring. So not one, but two ambulance men joined the party. Evening surgery had started, and the waiting room was filling up. The sight of an ambulance outside, with flashing blue lights, suggested to all comers that something exciting was up, and the receptionists explained that my evening surgery would be somewhat delayed. A hush descended on the building. Only Rita's efforts in the treatment room could be heard. There was a sense of excitement and anticipation. And then suddenly she was there—a beautiful baby girl, who cried lustily. And as those cries rang through the surgery, and reached the waiting room, there was an almost audible cheer. Certainly a letting out of communal bated breath. And everybody started to chat, and to laugh, and to celebrate. The ambulance man who had never witnessed a birth was almost in tears, as they gently loaded mother and baby into the ambulance to take them to hospital for postnatal care.

That special baby, 'our surgery baby', became even more special to me when Rita and Martin asked me to be godfather to her. And so I watched her grow up into the beautiful and talented young lady that she is today. Could anything be a greater privilege than that?

Amber was a sweet little girl, born just before Christmas. Her family lived just down the road from us, so when we, as a family, set out on our traditional carol-singing tour of the locality it seemed very right and appropriate to include Amber's home in our itinerary. We sallied forth into the snowy night, wrapped up in woolly scarves and hats, and carrying a paraffin lamp. Our musical efforts on the doorstep of Amber's house soon brought her parents to the door. They welcomed us in to the warm, and joined us in singing round Amber's cot. 'Silent night, holy night'. Like that first holy night in Bethlehem this night again was indeed, perhaps not silent, but most certainly holy, as we celebrated the miracle and the mystery of birth.

TILL DEATH

It was Woody Allen who said 'I am not afraid to die. I just don't want to be there when it happens.' Most people fear the process of dying, even if not death itself. Death has replaced sex as the taboo subject of conversation. But for a doctor, death is a reality that has to be faced day by day, and it is not just we who have to come to terms with it—it is our task to help others to come to terms with it. It may be with their own death, or with that of a loved one. Death can be said to be the one certainty in life, but it comes in many forms, and is coped with in many ways. The process of dying may be sudden and violent, or long and drawn out; it may be of a child, on the threshold of life, or of someone at the end of a long and well-lived life; it may be caused by illness, or it may be self-inflicted. It may bring with it feelings of anger, of indignation, of guilt, of regret, of fear, of loss, or of relief. The challenge for the family doctor is to meet people where they are, whether they be patients or loved ones, and to support them in a relevant way.

The hardest deaths are those of children. I think of the parents who had three children, each in turn born with a genetic problem that led, one by one, to death by the age of three or four years. The sheer agony that they went through, as each child in turn was diagnosed; their courage as they watched each child deteriorate; their dignity in the midst of broken-heartedness at each ending of a little life, were nothing but inspiring.

Jim was a young man with learning difficulties. He was his mother's one and only, the apple of her eye, and Beryl's whole life was devoted to him. Then he was diagnosed with cancer. Beryl's world fell apart. As Jim's condition deteriorated, and we fought to control his pain, it was hard to know sometimes which was the priority—helping Jim to understand what was going on, or supporting Beryl through times of anguish. There was no question of admitting Jim to hospital or hospice. His mother wanted her boy at home, and it was there that he died. She coped surprisingly well that night, but then came the difficulty of letting go. She would not allow his body to be removed from the home. The undertakers rose to the occasion, and dressed him in the very best. He lay in state, his bedroom decorated with all the things that had been precious to him— football scarves, music albums, posters, photographs. All the memories of happy days. It was summer, and there was concern about the state of the body as the warm days prior to the burial passed by. The day of the funeral was very difficult. Beryl could not bring herself to let go. She clung to Jim's body when the undertakers came for him, and she later tried to jump into the grave with the coffin. Her distress was extreme and overt. In the days that followed, I continued to visit her home, and she would show me the shrine that his bedroom had become. She said that sometimes Jim would come to her in the night. We talked a lot about the need to let go, and to remember that Jim rested in peace in God's care. Beryl did eventually come to terms with her loss, though I have no doubt that there always remained an aching void—that unfathomable void of a parent at the loss of a child.

'A light aircraft has crashed into woodland. Can you come immediately to the scene.' So came the urgent call from the police one Sunday afternoon. It was obvious from the abandoned police cars and ambulance that I had reached as far as a car could go. The tracks of a fire engine led through a cornfield and into a wood. I followed them at a run, not knowing what to expect. Tragically, the only role left for me was to certify death. A small aircraft had ploughed, nose first, through the trees and into the soft earth. A boy, no more than a teenager, was alone in the aircraft, still clutching the joystick. Death must have been instantaneous on impact. Stunned firemen and paramedics stood around. The thought in all our minds was 'How could this have happened? What a terrible waste of a young life!' It subsequently turned out that he was on his first solo flight, as an air cadet, and his friend, also on his first solo flight in another plane, had collided with him. The friend was able to limp his plane back to base. For this lad there had been no chance of survival. It was a salutary reminder of the risks and fragility of life, and somewhere was a family whose lives would never be the same again.

It was a busy morning in surgery when the call came from the emergency services. A young man had jumped into a flooded quarry at the foot of the hills, and had not surfaced. Would I, as duty doctor, attend immediately. It was a lake I knew well. When we first came to live here it was still a working quarry, the last on the hills—an ugly gouge out of the rocky hillside. Soon after, by act of Parliament, all quarrying was stopped. The deep pit was flooded, the surrounds landscaped, and a beautiful picnic spot created. But it had a drawback. On hot summer days the innocent-looking lake, with its blue-green water, attracted swimmers. And the water was very deep, very cold, and concealed underwater obstacles. On this occasion a party of foreign students, studying in a nearby city, had come for an outing. One had jumped in to the lake, and had not emerged. As I raced to the hills I wondered what I would do. At least twenty minutes had elapsed since he jumped. The scene that greeted me answered my question. The police and paramedics were already there, standing on the rocky edge of the lake, surveying the still water. A group of distraught friends of the missing man were pleading with the police to dive in and search for him, but they were forbidding and preventing anyone from doing so. By now any hopes of his survival were very small indeed, and they did not want any further deaths. They were awaiting a police diving team. It was no longer a case of rescue but of recovery. I felt for those students. It was natural to want somebody to do something. But sometimes there is nothing to do, and that is the wise decision. In due course, the young man's body was recovered. Sadly, it was by no means the last body to be recovered from that quarry lake.

For a parent to lose a child is tragedy. But also for a child to lose a parent. Helping a child through the pain of grief is a heart-breaking process, and how thankful we were for those charities set up to help this process. Jenny was aged eight, and her dad was dying from cancer. It would have been tempting to insulate her from the situation; perhaps to send her away to family or friends for a while; to tell her only part of the truth. But instead everyone was totally honest with her, and she helped her mother to care for him in his last days. At the end, when he was unconscious, we encouraged her to talk to him, and tell him how she was feeling. When she was not aware that anyone else was listening it was very moving to hear her say to him: 'Daddy, when you get to the end of your long train journey, will you wait for me at the station?' That was clearly how she had chosen to think of his death, as a journey, and a journey that she would one day take herself. It was a case of 'au revoir', and this helped her grieving.

Deaths, whether expected, or sudden and unexpected, cause wounds which, like ulcers, can take an awfully long time to heal. Sometimes, for the loved ones, a lot of the grieving has already been done before the death. They are prepared. Perhaps this is particularly so in the case of dementia. The loved one that they once knew has long since departed, perhaps no longer recognising their own spouse or relatives. They have become a shell of their former self, and a lot of the prolonged and agonising 'Goodbye' has already been said. But in the case of sudden death the grieving comes like a tornado, uprooting life and traumatising deeply. The classical stages of grief can last for many months, even years—shock and denial ('I just can't believe it . . .'); pain and guilt ('If only I had . . .'); anger ('They should have . . .'); depression and loneliness ('I just miss him or her so much!') and finally acceptance ('I must start to live again').

Perhaps the hardest kind of death to come to terms with is suicide. It seems so unnecessary. It needn't have been. And these feelings are often tied up with the guilt of the loved ones that they could, or should, have done more to prevent it. Over the years we experienced in the practice almost every kind of suicide—overdoses, hanging, shooting, the gas oven, exhaust fumes, wrist cutting, jumping from a height and deliberate drowning. I couldn't but admire the courage of some of those who took their own lives. What guts to do what they did! But then I realised that it was also sheer desperation. Life had become so utterly bleak, so utterly hopeless, that there seemed no alternative but to end it all. The thought of the mental torment they must have been through was very distressing.

Mr Morrison was prone to depression. He was a 'glass half empty' sort of person. I became used to his rather morose and pessimistic demeanour. When his wife became seriously ill he had good reason to feel low, and when she died any light that had been left in his life went out. He began to talk of life not being worth living—but he had said that before. I spoke with his family, and his daughter searched his house. We removed some potentially harmful tablets, and also—a totally unexpected finding—an unlicensed pistol, found hidden in his wardrobe. Two days later he took an overdose of tablets. Our search had obviously not been thorough enough. I sent him into hospital, and there, after recovering from the overdose, he was assessed by psychiatrists. In their opinion his behaviour was histrionic rather than that of clinical depression. He was discharged home after a few days. Mr Morrison was a skilled metal worker, and he had a well equipped workshop. It was his pride and joy. That night he fashioned a barrel out of a pipe, clamped it in a vice, and rigged up a firing pin that could be activated from the other end of the barrel. He produced some hidden ammunition. And, sitting on a stool in his workshop, he shot himself. I could almost hear him saying 'I told you I would, and nobody believed me!' Could we have done more? Can someone bent on suicide be prevented or dissuaded? How desperate he must have felt to go to such lengths to end his life. The tragedy of suicide leaves everybody feeling guilty, and in that sense it is a selfish act.

There were, however, deaths that could be said to be almost joyous. Mr and Mrs Newbold were in their nineties, and both had cancer. Both were dying. They lay side by side, holding hands in their double bed, as they had lain together over seventy years, and their lives gradually ebbed. They died within hours of one another. As the Bible says of David and Jonathan, 'In life they were loved and gracious, and in death they were not parted.' That is perhaps the way most of us would wish to die. Another 'good' death was that of Charles. He had cancer, and had come to terms with it. Clearly the end was not far away. On my way back from church on Christmas Day I popped in to see him. He was sitting up in bed, glass in hand, surrounded by family and friends, all drinking Bucks Fizz. I joined them, and we had a mini party. Two days later he died. His death was a celebration of life.

Although I was (and am) a licensed Lay Reader (now retitled a Licensed Lay Minister) in the Church of England, and was permitted therefore to conduct funerals, I chose not to. From time to time I was asked to, but always declined. Finding the time in working hours would have been difficult, and to agree to some and to refuse others would have been contentious. It would also have felt a bit odd to, as some might say, 'bury my failures.' So I was faced with a dilemma when Narindar asked me to conduct a simple Thanksgiving Service for the life of her husband, Sewa, and scattering of his ashes. Narindar and Sewa were of Indian origin, Sikhs who had both converted to Christianity. They were not patients of our practice. They had a ministry in a nearby town amongst the Asian community. We had established a link between our church and their community. Once a year about seventy of them—Sikhs, Hindus, Muslims and Christians—would come away from the grey town streets to our beautiful rural area, and we would give them a good day out. Some would climb the hills, some browse the shops, some enjoy a tranquil lake at the foot of the hills. Sewa always chose the lake, and his favourite spot in the world was to sit on a bench there, and watch the ducks on the water, and the green, bracken-clad hills beyond. When Sewa became ill with pancreatic cancer, and died, we lost a good friend. The funeral service and cremation were held at their home church, but Sewa had expressed a wish that his ashes be scattered on that lake at the foot of the hills. So it was that Narindar rang me. She wanted a simple committal service. She had rung our vicar first. He was away. Then the curate, but he was otherwise occupied. He suggested me. The difficulty was that I had no idea if it was permissible to scatter ashes on that lake. Was there some bye-law that forbade it? What if everyone wanted their ashes scattered on that water? Sometimes it is better not to enquire too deeply, or you discover answers that you don't want to hear. I knew what it would have meant to Sewa, and to Narindar, so agreed. We fixed on a date and a time. A group mainly of Asians would come from the town. A group would come from our church. We would meet at the lake, and have a short and simple service.

As soon as I arrived at the lake on the appointed day I realised that it was not going to be so simple. Every few yards around the perimeter of the lake was a fisherman! A fishing competition was in progress! A quick reconnoitre established that the water at the far side was too shallow for fishing, and, moreover, a small island with a clump of trees made that bit of shore quite discreet. But it meant that we would all have to walk round the lake. By now car loads of ladies in bright saris were arriving. And car loads of our church members were also arriving. This was not going to be a quiet, discreet event!

The fishermen watched with fascination as this colourful, cosmopolitan procession made its way round the lake. Their quizzical glances conveyed the question 'What on earth is going on?' As we arrived at the far shore I became aware of a group of people clearing bracken about a hundred yards away. They too paused in their exertions, and surveyed this unusual procession. They obviously had some sort of official connection with the area. Did they know of a bye-law that we were about to break? A further problem arose. Ducks! As soon as they saw us gathering near the far bank every duck on the pond headed for us, expecting to partake of a lavish picnic. In my mind I had visions of Sewa's ashes being gobbled up by the ducks as fast as we scattered them. Some improvisation was required.

'Has anyone brought a picnic?' I asked. Yes, someone had.

'May I have a couple of sandwiches?' I asked.

We had a reading and a prayer. The fishermen watched from across the pond. The bracken-clearers watched. I said a few words about how much Sewa's life had meant to so many, and how special that spot had been to him. Then I turned to the small group of children who had come. 'Now' I said, 'You and I are going to feed the ducks with these sandwiches, while the grown-ups scatter Sewa's ashes on the water.'

The children and I walked a little way along the bank, followed by a quacking flotilla. Meanwhile the scattering of the ashes was done in peace, and Sewa's mortal remains dispersed in this place he loved. His soul, we knew, was safe with his Lord, and so our lakeside foray was not a sad occasion, but a celebration. We made our way back to the cars, this multi-ethnic, multicoloured procession, chatting happily in a variety of languages. Did the competing fishermen and the bracken-clearers realise that that day a good man had won the ultimate prize?

FOR BETTER, FOR WORSE

Eileen Rowland was quite a formidable lady who didn't take 'no' for an answer. In her eighties, she had already had three husbands, all of whom had died, possibly from exhaustion. She was prone to sending me scrappy type-written notes to keep me abreast of her latest symptoms. It was a Tuesday when one of her missives arrived at the surgery, but this time it was not an update on the performance of her body. It was an invitation. On the very next Friday, just three days hence, she was getting married. This was complete news to me, and probably quite recent news to her intended. He was Jim Woods, a lovely, gentle widower.

At that stage I had not actually met Jim, but knew of him through one of the other partners, George. George was convinced that Jim must be a very unwilling victim in this proposed match. Neither of us felt any doubt as to who had made the proposal.

The letter went on. It was more than just an invitation. It was a request—verging on a demand—that I should be, in effect, best man to Jim (whom, as mentioned, I had never met), and that my wife Rosemary would be, in effect, bridesmaid to Eileen. As my mind began to search desperately for the excuse of some pre-arranged and unmissable appointment at whatever time the wedding was to take place I read on.

'Will you please choose the time of the wedding—whenever you are free—and let me and the vicar know.'

There was no easy get-out.

Friday dawned. The time of my choosing was after morning surgery, at 12.30. We met another two couples making their way, somewhat reluctantly, up the path to the village church. That made a congregation of six. A lady from the village was out walking her dog in the churchyard. She knew both Eileen and Jim, but knew nothing about the imminent matrimony. We persuaded her to join us, swelling the congregation to seven and a dog. I met Jim for the first time in the church porch. He looked somewhat strained, and it crossed my mind that my medical services might be required before the afternoon was out. Jim fumbled in his pocket and, producing the ring, handed it to me as the best man. Rosemary was greatly relieved to find that her role as bridesmaid was minimal. There was no train, no bouquet to care for, in fact nothing to do.

The vicar arrived, rather red-faced and breathless. One got the feeling that this was an interruption in his flock-tending duties that he did not altogether welcome. As he began to recite the opening words of the marriage service a pigeon that had been trapped in the church decided to do some fairly low fly-pasts. This excited the dog, and rather distracted all of us, not least the bride and groom, from concentrating on the vicar's words about the purpose of marriage. The vicar, rather flustered, forgot to miss out the bit about procreation of children, and I hoped that this would not raise the hopes of this eighty year old couple. But then after all, there was the precedent of Sarah in the Bible. She was 'well past the age of childbearing' when she conceived Isaac . . . but I pulled my straying thoughts together. The vicar seemed to have got stuck on a particular line in the service, and Eileen had collapsed in giggles. He was asking her to repeat some words after him, and she was not responding. He repeated again: 'Will you, Eileen, say after me: "I, Eileen, take thee, Jim, to be my wedded wife"?'

No reply from Eileen, just more giggles.

The pigeon did another low fly-pass, and the dog tried to take off to join it.

The vicar tried again, but by now Eileen was helpless with laughter, and we had all joined in. The service was degenerating into a farce.

'Husband! To be my husband!' she managed to blurt out between her giggles. And the red-faced vicar corrected himself. By the end of the service we were all reasonably convinced that Eileen and Jim were now, for better or worse, man and wife, and that we had got it the right way round.

It would be gratifying to say that Eileen and Jim lived happily ever after. It is perhaps better to draw the curtains on that one. But marriages late in life do sometimes work out well, and do provide a beautiful and gentle companionship in the twilight of life.

Mr Wenham was something of a baby-snatcher. He was aged ninety-eight when he married his bride of just eighty-four. It was his third marriage. He had got to know his bride from giving her lifts to the surgery—he felt that running the 'old folk' around was something that he could do for the community. It never seemed to cross his mind that he was himself, more than most, one of those 'old folk'. A memorable day was Mr Wenham's one hundredth birthday. For some reason he had never received four medals that he had won for service in the First World War. The Colonel of his old regiment came that day, and presented him with the medals, and the regimental band played in the day room of his block of flats. With medals and a telegram from the Queen he was a proud man, and deservedly so.

I am a great believer in marriage. Perhaps that is easily said by one who has been blessed with a very happy marriage, and a wonderful family. But surely it is an ideal that most of us would aspire to. Marriage brings stability to a family, and also to society. It brings security to children. Stable marriages, secure families, are the building blocks of a healthy society. I am traditional enough to hold to the definition of marriage as the union of one man with one woman, exclusively and for life. Of course life does not always take a smooth and ideal pathway, and there has to be room for mistakes, regrets, and new starts. But that does not negate the ideal. No couple, on their wedding day, expect ever to fall out of love, or anticipate a messy end to their marriage. They expect only the best. Life is full of promise. What they do not always realise is that their marriage will have to be worked at, nurtured. There will have to be apologies and forgiveness. There will have to be compromises. Good marriages don't just happen. For this reason for many years Rosemary and I have been involved, through church, in marriage preparation days for couples, looking at the main reasons for marriages going wrong—poor communication, loss of intimacy, and disagreements over money. To be forewarned is to be forearmed. Prevention is better than cure. Problems can be nipped in the bud, provided the couple are willing. Our marriage preparation days were designed to help engaged couples to develop good communication, to learn ways of keeping love and intimacy alive, and to develop healthy financial strategies. Over the years I saw in surgery many people with problems stemming from tensions within their marriage.

Increasingly couples are not willing to commit to marriage. They are happy to remain as partners. Ros and Peter were in that situation. He actually wanted to tie the knot, to make an act of commitment, and he told me so. But Ros didn't see the point.

'To get married would be as though we owned each other,' she said to me. 'We love one another. We live together. Isn't that enough? I don't want to feel tied down.'

But then the day came when Ros showed up in surgery in floods of tears.

'Pete has left me,' she cried. 'I can't believe it! We went on holiday with friends, and he and she started an affair, and now he's gone off with her. He's left me!' She was distraught.

I was tempted to say 'But isn't this what you wanted—freedom, lack of ties, no commitment?'

I didn't say it—it would have been cruel to do so. Nor would we ever know if things might have been different if they had committed to one another in marriage. But it set me thinking again about the importance—and the cost, and the discipline—of total commitment. And the importance of admitting that we are sometimes wrong, and need to say 'Sorry!' Perhaps one of the most misguided quotes comes in the film *Love Story*, 'Love is never having to say sorry.' That may be true for perfect beings, but for ordinary mortals 'Love is being prepared often to say sorry.'

It was the young folk, and their children, that worried me most. It seemed that so many entered into relationships so casually, with little thought for the implications of what they were doing, or of the long-term perspective. Perhaps marriage, partnerships, sex, have been affected by our consumer society, in which we expect to buy and to have whatever we want now, immediately—the plastic card society. And likewise in relationships. Patience, waiting, wooing, courtship are all so old-fashioned. I want 'it' now. And so young couples, with little experience of life, move in together, and before long a baby is on the way. But parenting is, of course, tough and exhausting. Romance goes by the board, and at the first hurdle the relationship breaks up. And life moves on to the next relationship. I knew young women with several children, each of whom had a different surname—the fruit of successive relationships. How do those children grow up with any sense of stability? Where and to whom do they belong? Where is the role model of parenting and family life that will enable them to develop mature and stable relationships when they grow up? But attempt to say any of this to them and they would give me the glazed look of a tourist gazing at an Egyptian antiquity. Had I come from another planet? I fear for the future stability of our society.

DAY BY DAY

The countryside has a pulse of its own, a rhythm, a cycle. This was the familiar and reassuring background to life. The seasons came and went, and each one had its beauty. Spring brought snowdrops in profusion, and banks of primroses. Newborn lambs leapt for joy in the green fields, and the birdsong heralded the long lost warmth of the sun. Soon the hills were smothered in a blue haze as millions of bluebells nodded their heads and filled the clean air with their scent. Spring would merge into summer, season of green growing fields and bracken turning golden on the hills; the time for the waspish buzz of mowers and the tangy smell of barbecues and bonfires. And then suddenly the days would be drawing in again, and there would be an evening chill in the air. The trees, bored with their shades of green, would subtly don their autumn glory. The combine harvesters would be out, day and night, gathering in the ripened grain. We would hear the excited voices of children out in the lane, come to collect the enormous shiny conkers dropping from the ancient horse chestnut trees. The winter too had its beauty—a vista of floods, creeping across the marsh below us, and the honking of flocks of geese heading for their winter feeding grounds. Sometimes a blanket of snow would cover the land, the white horizon merging into the grey sky, and there would be a hush, as though the earth was waiting in expectancy for God to say something. This was the canvas on which the activities of everyday life were painted. This backdrop to a fulfilling life just added to the sense of gratitude and joy.

We, at our home, in its elevated position on a ridge, could look down on the regular winter floods, and enjoy the expanse of water. The marsh below our house is a flood plain for the river. Plans to turn it into a reservoir had long since been dropped, and the floods came and went each winter, relieving the river of some of its deluge. But never was there any threat to us. We were well above the floods. It was a very different story for those living close to the river. Every winter they lived in dread of the rising waters inundating their houses. It is not just the flood water that is so devastating, nor just the fear, or the smell and the filth, but also the aftermath—the long process of cleaning up, and drying out, and making insurance claims (if the property was even insurable), and re-equipping, and re-decorating. Many of the houses were, in due course, protected by flood barriers—at first temporary, and then permanent. But the water has to go somewhere, and the roads in and out of the village could not be protected. The first winter of the new millennium saw the approach road to the river bridge under two feet of water. To visit our many patients who lived on the other side of the river entailed an eighteen-mile detour. The army came to the rescue, ferrying us over in their high lorries, and acting as a shuttle service for those who needed to come over to the village. It felt grand arriving to do a cross-river home visit in an enormous army truck, complete with driver and paramedic, and a ladder to descend by.

The winter of 1982 brought with it snow and blizzards the like of which hadn't been seen for years. The landscape disappeared under a blanket of white. The lane to our house was buried under several feet of snow, which reached from hedge top to hedge top. I was trapped at home for two days. While David and George went out together from the surgery on essential visits in a borrowed four-wheel drive vehicle, I took all phone calls, and gave advice to patients as appropriate. Few could have got to the surgery anyway. When the blizzard finally relented, our neighbouring farmer carved a narrow track through the drifts with his tractor. I was able to drive down this glistening tunnel, the sides of which were higher than the car, hoping against hope that I would not meet another vehicle.

It was that winter which finally decided the source of our water at home. In East Africa, our water had been pumped from a deep borehole by a six horsepower Lister diesel engine. It was my responsibility to keep that engine working. No engine, no water! Many a time, as I cranked repeatedly to get the old machine started, and as I struggled with cylinder heads and worn valves, I would say to Rosemary, 'What I look forward to more than anything, when we eventually return to live in England, is just to turn on a tap, and have an endless supply of pure water! No temperamental diesel engine to nurse into life!'

So it was ironical that when we bought our dream house in England the water came from a well, and it was pumped by—yes!—a six horsepower Lister diesel engine, identical to the one we had in Africa, and just as temperamental. That 1982 winter was, for me, the last straw. The pipes froze, the storage tank sprang leaks, the engine frequently and stubbornly refused to start. I had had enough, and we had our house connected to the water mains. Wells and pumps are a lovely idea, but come a severe winter and the romance palls.

Against this backdrop memories stand out like islands in a vast ocean. We look back and we remember the highlights, projecting like rocks from the waters of time. We remember the things that are memorable—the happy days, the sunny days, the crises. But the day to day routine, the humdrum of life, becomes blurred and forgotten. Likewise, in a personal diary, the highlights of life are recorded, but not the routine background to life. To record 'Just another busy day' is of no interest. Yet that is what most of life consisted of—busy days, often exhausting days, and a succession of patients with relatively minor illnesses. A normal day consisted of morning and evening surgeries, at both of which each partner might see twenty or more patients, and then came a number of home visits, and perhaps an antenatal or child health or school clinic. By the end of an average day I was likely to have seen fifty or sixty patients. In the early days we started work at 8 am, finished morning surgery at about twelve midday, did home visits or clinics until 6 pm, and then began evening surgery. We were lucky to get home before 8.30 pm. One night in three we were on call, and also one weekend in three. We each had a half day off during the week. Sometimes the work seemed relentless, especially if the nights and weekends were busy. When we invited Sue, our trainee at the time, to join us as a fourth partner the load was spread a bit, and more so when Julian became our fifth partner.

As the number of our patients grew, from about eight to twelve thousand, so the practice staff and facilities grew. Three times we extended the surgery. We took on more receptionists, and appointed a practice manager; we introduced practice nurses and in time a phlebotomist; secretaries, a telephonist, and a caretaker followed. We were a dispensing practice. In the early days we partners did the dispensing, which took time between each patient. So we appointed a dispenser, and in due course a qualified pharmacist and assistants. What had been a small, family-like practice was in danger of becoming a rather impersonal, busy, high-powered business. It would have been very easy to lose the personal touch, and for us all to become stressed and irritable. Something that I believe helped to prevent that was humour. So long as we could laugh together, and sometimes have fun, stress levels remained manageable.

Red Nose Day was always marked by the staff, not just by wearing red noses, but also by dressing up. The theme one year was pirates. I shall not forget the expression on the face of a new patient, as he was registered by a receptionist with a patch over one eye and a toy parrot on her shoulder. His expression said 'Have I come to the right place? Is it safe?' Significant milestones were often marked by the staff. On my sixtieth birthday I arrived at the surgery to discover that, overnight, my consulting room had been turned into a tropical jungle. A palm tree overhung my desk. Creepers were entwined on the curtains. A large black gorilla was sitting in the patient's chair. Monkeys swung from the lights, and a lion (wearing a notice that said 'I'm ready when you are, doc!') was awaiting examination on my couch. The jungle theme remained all day, and most patients loved it, and entered into the fun of the occasion. But I do recall one rather humourless man who coped by ignoring it all. He sat primly alongside the gorilla, without appearing to notice it. Perhaps he thought that, for this mad doctor, everything and anything was as to be expected. When a retired banker and his wife came to register with the practice on another occasion, and were asked which partner they wanted to register with, they replied, 'With whoever will make us laugh most!' Apparently the receptionists recommended me—a reputation I had to live up to whenever the banker or his wife came to see me. There is certainly truth in the saying that 'laughter is the best medicine'.

A local councillor came to the reception desk one day. The receptionist was busy negotiating a wheelchair round the waiting area. It contained an apparently frail and disabled patient. She called over to the councillor:

'Can I help you?'

'Yes, I have come to register with the practice, please.'

'Certainly! Jane will do that for you.'

Whereupon the frail, disabled 'patient' leapt from the wheel chair and took her place at the desk. She was Jane! In a quiet moment the two of them had been practising their wheel chair skills.

'I'm very impressed!' said the councillor. 'If this practice can produce miraculous recoveries like that I know I have come to the right place!'

Not quite so sudden and miraculous was the recovery of a temporary patient. She was a friend of Jean, one of my regulars, and she had become very ill, and unable to care for herself. She came to stay with Jean, and over the course of several weeks I visited her frequently. At first she was bed-bound, and very weak, but very gradually she began to improve, until she could sit up for short periods. A doctor friend had come to stay with us, and was with me one day in the village when we met Jean, pushing her friend in a wheelchair. It was her first outing for a long time, and a great step forwards, though she still looked exceedingly frail.

'Look at her!' Jean said to me excitedly. 'Another of your successes!'

When they had gone from earshot my doctor friend turned to me and said: 'Gosh! If she is one of your successes, I would hate to see your failures!'

I hadn't had much success with Anne. She had osteoarthritis of her knees—the legacy of many years of lugging children and scrubbing floors. We had tried painkillers, and anti-inflammatory gels and tablets, and physiotherapy. Nothing made any significant difference, and the possible need for surgery arose. Then one day she came into my consulting room with a broad smile on her face.

'I've found a cure for my knees doctor,' she said.

'Oh wonderful!' I said. 'What's the secret?'

'It is a secret. I can't tell you.'

'Why ever not? I would love to know what it is that has helped.'

'If I tell you, you would only laugh.'

'Laugh? I won't laugh. If it works I'd like to know, seriously.'

She paused, then a bit red-faced said, 'It's WD40. I spray them each day with WD40!'

I am sorry to say that I laughed. The thought of spraying fine oil, the treatment for rusty hinges, onto the outside of a joint seemed bizarre. But for Anne it worked, and what else matters? I heard subsequently of other people who have used WD40 on worn-out joints, with success. If it works it works! There are not always logical explanations in medicine. It is an art as much as a science. The mind has enormous power over the body. And maybe, just maybe, WD40 does have some mysterious ability to penetrate and to lubricate worn out joints.

Many a time I thanked God for the gift of laughter—for the ability to laugh at myself, and to see the ridiculous side of life. I kept a record of funny sayings, usually due to the inadvertent misuse of a word, or misunderstanding as to how the body functions. There was the old lady who complained that her iron tablets were causing her to be 'consummated'. A husband, whose wife was having urinary problems, said: 'I hope you don't mind my mentioning it, doctor, but don't you think her problem might be due to her prostate?'

A lady who had just had an operation assured me that her husband had just been given two weeks 'passionate leave'. Another, who was trying to conceive, said that she had been given 'infidelity tablets'. In the case of a further couple, who were trying to conceive, the husband had been somewhat reluctant and embarrassed to produce a sample. But all was well when the wife said, 'I twisted his arm and he produced it.' This was a technique new to science!

A lady surveyed the photos of our children, that graced my consulting room, and said, 'Aren't they all so good-looking?'

'Yes, I think so,' I replied modestly.

'They must take after their mother,' she said.

On occasion, when a feral child was taking my consulting room apart, or when a mother with no idea about parenting was shouting empty threats at an oblivious little terrorist, the old-fashioned, authorised version of the Bible's use of the word 'suffer' seemed very appropriate. 'Suffer little children.' But of course the word Jesus used meant 'let' or 'allow'. 'Let the little children come to me, and do not hinder them, for the Kingdom of God belongs to such as these.' It is the innocence, the naivety, the honesty of little children that is so appealing. I loved to treat children. The first challenge, of course, was to win their confidence, so as to allow an examination of some sort to take place. Here I found it important to speak to the child themselves (assuming they were old enough to understand), and not to speak to the parents about them, over their heads. Allowing them to have a go with the stethoscope would often engage their interest, and distract them from destroying my room. I would sometimes recruit them as helpers. Syringing of a parent's ears (an effective procedure now rarely done, and anyway now delegated to a nurse) was always a popular occasion.

I would ask the child to watch the parent's opposite ear very carefully, and to tell me the moment they saw water coming out of it. This ensured rapt concentration by the child—and disappointment that the water never did seem to reach the opposite ear. An array of toys were also useful distractions for small children—until the health police ruled that toys, and soft toys in particular, were a source of cross-infection, and must no longer be provided. I cannot remember a single instance when a child picked up an infection in that way—though toys probably boosted the immunity of many a child.

To my surprise, the Richards told me that they would be leaving the practice as they were moving to France. My surprise was because, to my knowledge, they had never been to France.

They did not strike me as being Francophiles, nor to be the sort of people who would enjoy another culture. They lived happily in a pleasant little bungalow. They had always seemed very content. I wished them well, and we said our goodbyes. A few weeks later they were back in the surgery, having signed on again.

'But I thought you were moving to live in France,' I said.

'Well, we did, but we didn't like it there. You see everyone was speaking French, and we don't speak French. And we found that they drive on the right, which we are not used to. So we have come back.'

Doctors are supposed to have a certain dignity—or so I am told. A presence. An air of calm and authority. The 'Trust me, I'm a doctor!' aura. Of course, often when we look calm and confident and knowledgeable we are in fact, like the proverbial swan, paddling furiously below the surface. The age of the internet often means that patients know far more about an obscure illness than we do, when they come seeking advice. So it is good from time to time to be cut down to size. After I had examined an elderly lady in a nursing home, and had listened to her heart and chest, she asked, 'Are you a doctor?'

'Yes, I am' I replied.

'Well you don't look like one.'

'So what do I look like, Gertie?' I asked.

'You look like a scavenger.'

We took our grandchildren one year to their first pantomime. Clearly they needed some grandfatherly coaching and advice as to how to get involved in the show. I set an example. 'Look behind you!' I bellowed. 'Oh yes it is!' 'Boooooo!' and so on. It seemed right to help them to get into the spirit of the story. The next day in surgery, a patient said, 'Dr Webster, I was sitting just behind you at the pantomime last night. I shall never think of you in the same way again!' She didn't elaborate. She didn't need to.

DOCTOR ON HOLIDAY

Something that I guess most doctors dread is that call over the P.A. system 'Is there a doctor in the house?' or 'Would any doctor on board please make themselves known.' We were flying with a group from our church to Israel, and I was dozing in my seat when I received a sharp prod.

'Aren't you going?'

'Going where?' I asked, coming to with a jolt.

'They are calling for a doctor at the front of the plane. Someone has collapsed.'

I made my way somewhat reluctantly up the aisle, and there ahead was what looked like a mini medical congress. A rather large lady, red faced and sweaty, was surrounded by about a dozen doctors. They were trying to decide who should best examine and treat her. 'I am a cardiologist!' one said. 'I am a neurologist!' said another. 'I am a surgeon!' 'I am an oncologist!' As I stood on the fringe of this illustrious gathering I thought to myself 'Well, I'm just a humble GP, and maybe it is I who should decide which of you to refer her to.' As I say, that's what I thought to myself, but I said nothing. Instead, like a coward, I crept back to my seat, leaving her in the hands of a committee capable of treating her for whatever ailment she chose to mention.

It is very tempting, when off duty or on holiday, to keep

one's medical profession under wraps. But, of course, it is only right to do so if alternative care and treatment is available. In one sense, a doctor is never off duty. When driving to town one day I came across a cyclist in the ditch. He had just been knocked by a car, which failed to stop. I rang for an ambulance, and meanwhile checked him for injuries. I had just completed my examination, and ruled out anything serious, when another car screeched to a halt, a young man leapt out, and pushing me aside said, 'It's OK! I'll take over! I've got my first aid certificate!'

'Thank goodness for that,' I said, and left him to wait for the ambulance. For him it was an opportunity to put his new-found skills into practice, and he didn't need to know that I was a doctor.

When on holiday in Britain, it is perfectly possible to remain anonymous. Abroad it is more difficult, because the 'doctor' title appears in one's passport, and it is usually under that title that one has been registered. On a number of occasions I have been called on to see sick or injured people, and not least in the Maldives, where only a few of the larger islands have a resident doctor. We were holidaying one year on Velidhu. It was idyllic—beaches of white, powdery sand, and warm, blue-green sea. We were stretched out under a palm tree, totally relaxed and unwound. The practice seemed very, very far away, and I was catching up with rest and sleep. Then we heard footsteps approaching across the sand. I cautiously opened one eye. It was the island manager. 'Are you Doctor Webster?'

'Er—yes,' I replied, somewhat cautiously.

'Please can you help me doctor. I have a problem with some guests.'

A German family, father, mother and three-year-old daughter, had just arrived on the island. As they arrived the news came through to them from Germany that a kindergarten friend of their daughter, a little boy with whom she had been playing twenty-four hours previously, had just died from fulminating meningococcal meningitis. Their daughter was a close contact, and at serious risk. The family were, understandably, distraught. They were demanding that the manager arrange for them to be flown immediately, by seaplane, to the capital, Male, in order to catch an international flight back to Germany. The manager was trying to explain to them that, as it was late evening and would soon be dark, neither a seaplane nor a speedboat was possible, because of the many reefs. Only a slow, local fishing boat, a *dhoni*, was possible, and that would take all night.

I sat the Germans down, and explained to them that the next forty-eight hours were critical for their daughter. The last place she needed to be, if she was taken ill, was mid-flight, or mid-ocean, between the Maldives and Germany. What we needed, I explained, was to get a prophylactic antibiotic, Rifampicin, for her. I said I would ring a doctor on Male, and try to arrange for some to be brought on a *dhoni* overnight. So began a series of phone calls to Male. Rifampicin is used to treat tuberculosis, and there is a huge problem with drug resistance in the treatment of tuberculosis. The ruling by the medical authorities in the Maldives was that only the Minister of Health could authorise the use of Rifampicin for anything other than tuberculosis. So it was that I found myself speaking to the Maldives Minister of Health at his home. He agreed to its use in this exceptional case, and the Medical Officer of Health in charge of infectious diseases was roused from his home to take a bottle of Rifampicin syrup to the docks, to be put on a *dhoni* that would bring it to Velidhu overnight. The arrival time was estimated to be 6 am. I promised the German parents that I would meet the *dhoni*, and bring the antibiotic to their cottage. Meanwhile, they were to call me if they were worried about their little girl, Marie Lisa.

At midnight there was a banging on the door of our bungalow. It was the German father.

'Doctor! Doctor! You must come. Marie Lisa is very hot. She is not well.'

We made our way through the moonlit palm trees to their cottage. As we entered I was struck by the overpowering heat in the room—they had turned the air conditioning off.

'We were afraid that she might get cold,' they explained.

Meanwhile, Marie Lisa, red and sweaty, was leaping happily all over the beds. A quick check-over revealed no sinister signs. We put the air conditioning back on, and I returned to our cottage.

An hour passed, and I had just got off to sleep when there was, again, a loud banging on our door. My heart sank. If Marie Lisa did take ill I had nothing to treat her with. But it was not the German father. It was an English man, on his honeymoon.

'Sorry to bother you,' he said. 'But I understand that you are a doctor. My wife has got terrible cystitis. She is in agony, and passing blood.'

Off we set, through the palm trees, and along the walkway to their luxury water bungalow. The full moon reflected on the limpid sea. His wife was indeed in agony, with a severe attack of honeymoon cystitis. I had suitable antibiotics for her, and with advice about copious drinking, I returned once more to bed.

The alarm woke me at 5.45 am. I donned shorts and flip-flops and made my way to the jetty. There sure enough was the *dhoni*, making its way slowly through the reef, and bearing the precious bottle of Rifampicin. I went straight round to the Germans' cottage, and administered the first dose to Marie Lisa. The parents breathed an audible sigh of relief. There seemed little point in returning to bed, so I did a 'ward round' instead, and made an early morning call on the honeymooners. Astonishingly, she was already feeling very much better, and her gratitude was profuse. During the coming days, we would frequently meet Marie Lisa with her parents, and each time they would thrust her into my arms 'just to check that she is OK'.

And she remained very well, and they were able to continue their holiday with increasingly less anxiety. The island manager presented me with a plate that said I was an 'honoured guest'. The real reward though was in seeing the smiling faces of those German parents, and of little Marie Lisa.

A less happy outcome was on another holiday on Velidhu. Mohammed was the Maldivian in charge of our cottage. He saw to our needs, and decorated our bed each night with beautiful arrangements of bougainvillea and flamboyant tree flowers. At some point he discovered that I was a doctor, and he asked if he could make an appointment to see me. I rather dreaded that I would be asked to treat some condition for which I did not have any medicine. But it was not about himself. It was about his child. Mohammed had married a girl from Vellore in South India. She was still young when she had their first child, a son, and it had been a long and very difficult labour. He was a big boy. He was the apple of Mohammed's eye—what more could a father ask for than a son? Wife and son had remained in India, and from time to time Mohammed would visit them. But it became obvious, as he grew, that he had not reached the usual milestones. By then he was three years old, and he could not sit unsupported; he had never stood, and, of course, could not walk. Moreover, his speech was limited. He had to be fed, and he was incontinent. Mohammed showed me photos of his son, and it seemed very obvious from them that he had cerebral palsy, presumably from brain injury at birth.

'We have taken him to many doctors in India, and they have given us many different medicines for him, and taken all our money, but still he is no better,' explained Mohammed.

How do you explain to a father that his much-loved son is not better because medicines cannot make him better? I explained the nature of cerebral palsy to Mohammed, and that what they needed to seek was, not a cure, but help for his son to live as full a life as possible. I told him about Vellore Christian

Hospital in South India, which has an excellent reputation for care. I felt sure that there they would not be ripped off, but would get honest advice. His hopes of one day bringing his wife and son to his home island in the Maldives seemed very unlikely to happen. How do you push a wheel chair in soft sand? What do you do when you need medical help on a remote island? I felt that I had snuffed out Mohammed's hopes, but he was grateful to know the truth.

'Inshallah! God's will be done!' he said, with Muslim fatalism.

It was a holiday on Cyprus that presented the biggest challenges. We went with a Christian holiday organisation, a group of about thirty of us. Each day began, for those who wished, with prayers at 8.30 am. One member of the group, Terry, had come without his wife, and with the intention of doing some long walks.

'Could we have prayers a bit earlier, at 8 am?' he asked Chris, the leader of the group. 'That would give me a bit longer in the day for walking.'

It was agreed by all. But the following morning Terry was not at prayers, which seemed odd, as he was the one who had asked for the earlier start. Nor did he come to breakfast. Chris rang his room, but there was no reply.

'Perhaps he decided to make a really early start,' I suggested, but Chris felt uneasy.

'Would you come with me to his room, just to check?' he said.

We explained to the manager, and borrowed a key to Terry's room. Chris's worst fears were realised—Terry was on the bathroom floor, propped up against the washbowl, and dead. His body was cold, and rigor mortis had set in. He must have died early in the night. We left everything as it was, and went to break the news.

The manager was most upset. This was not good for his hotel. But then he turned to me.

'You are a doctor, yes?'

'Yes!'

'Then you can write a death certificate, yes?'

'No! I cannot write a certificate. I don't know Terry. I met him for the first time yesterday. I have no knowledge of his medical background. I have no idea why he died. In the UK, this death has to be reported to the police, who will inform the coroner. I think you should tell the police.'

At the word 'police' the manager winced visibly, and I had to persuade him that there was no alternative. I could not, and would not, write a death certificate. The police came, and were taken upstairs to view the body. I then went through the same conversation with them—'I was a doctor, yes? I would write a certificate, yes?'

'No!'

It was finally agreed that Terry should be taken to the hospital mortuary for a post-mortem examination.

The problem then arose of how to get Terry out of the hotel discretely, without alarming the other guests. Because he had died sitting up, and because rigor mortis had set in, we could not straighten the body. The manager had visions of wheeling out a shrouded body in a wheel chair. My mind turned to Fawlty Towers.

'Do you have one of those large laundry baskets on wheels?' I asked the manager.

And so Chris and I lifted Terry gently into a laundry basket, covered him with sheets, and wheeled him along the corridors, and down the lift, without raising so much as a glance from passing guests. Although I hardly knew him, I think Terry would have been amused. Post-mortem showed a ruptured aortic aneurysm, so death would have been swift, and nothing would have saved him. Chris had the sad task of ringing his widow in England to break the news.

That was not the end of my medical adventures on that Cyprus holiday. On the last evening, at dinner, an English couple were sitting at a table a little way from us. The man began to cough, and at first I thought nothing of it until I realised that he was turning blue. He wasn't coughing—he was choking. I leapt to my feet and rushed to do the Heimlich manoeuvre, but another man, at an adjacent table, beat me to it. Up came the offending piece of meat, the patient gave a huge breath, and recovered consciousness. He left the dining room to compose himself. His rescuer just sat down nonchalantly and continued his meal, as though this was a pretty standard activity for dinner time. When the patient returned, now composed and pink again, he headed straight for me, and I realised that I was the last person he saw before he lost consciousness. He squeezed my shoulder and took my hand.

'Thanks ever so much mate,' he said. 'You saved my life!'

I redirected him to his true rescuer, and wondered to myself who he was. He reacted so promptly, and did a perfect job. Perhaps he too was a doctor incognito—or, more likely, a paramedic; or maybe someone who had just got his first aid certificate!

Our usual holiday destination for many years—and still now—is the beautiful little Channel Island of Sark. The tidal range in these islands is huge, and the currents are strong and potentially dangerous. But when our host offered to take us all out on a trip round the island in his speed boat, and to give our daughter an opportunity to water ski, we happily agreed. We were rounding the southern tip of Little Sark when we noticed someone standing on the rocky shore, waving to us. As we went inshore we recognised Philip, an islander and resident of Little Sark. At that time he was doing his stint as island constable. He had a coil of rope over his shoulder, and he looked worried.

'A lady has reported that her husband has fallen down a cliff on Little Sark,' he shouted. 'She is very distressed, and can't remember exactly where it happened. Have you seen anyone?'

We realised that it would be quite impossible to carry him up the cliffs. The best direction for rescue would be from the sea. Our host had his mobile phone, and he rang the emergency services in Guernsey. The ambulance boat, the Flying Christine, was dispatched immediately. Soon we saw it, surging through the choppy sea. But then a new problem presented itself. The Flying Christine was too big to go all the way inshore. An inflatable dinghy was launched to reach the rocks. The paramedics made our casualty comfortable, and very gingerly we carried him on a stretcher across the slippery rocks. We inverted the dinghy, and laid the stretcher on its bottom. Two of us then knelt astride the stretcher, and paddled the inverted dinghy out to the Flying Christine. The wind had got up a bit, and as I paddled with one hand I clung to the stretcher with the other—to have our patient slip off would have been unfortunate! Yet another problem arose when we arrived at the ambulance boat. The paramedic and I stood to lift the stretcher onto the Flying Christine, but every time we lifted it, instead of the stretcher rising, the inverted dinghy sank into the water. Finally, with the help of a few more hands on the ambulance boat we hauled him safely aboard.

There was to be no water skiing that day. On arrival back at Sark's little Creux Harbour, I went in search of the casualty's wife, to tell her what had happened. She later said that X-rays had confirmed that both his heel bones had been shattered. Several years later, I happened to meet the lady again, on Sark. She said that it had taken her husband nearly a year to recover, and to regain his mobility, but then, very sadly, he had died suddenly from a heart attack. She held no grudges against Sark and its potentially dangerous coast. She had come back to relive happy memories of times there with her husband.

CREATURES GREAT AND SMALL

I like animals. Or perhaps I should say that I like animals that live with us. I do not always like other people's animals. Most dogs are friendly and welcoming, but not all. Some regard the doctor's visit as an invasion of their territory, a threat to the well-being of their owners. Perhaps they are right! It is the large, fierce-looking dogs that unnerve me.

I was called one night to a remote house. As I parked on the drive I noticed in the headlights two enormous hounds sitting on the lawn. They were, I believe, Rhodesian Ridgebacks, otherwise known as 'Lion Dogs', bred and used in Africa for lion hunting. As the car drew to a stop they rose to their feet, and watched me intently. I estimated that about thirty yards lay between me and the kitchen door. Thirty yards also lay between me and the dogs. Who was faster? But I knew that I must not run, nor show any sign of fear. I eased myself out of the car, and, with one eye on the dogs and one on the door, I walked up the path. The dogs let out low growls, and one of them moved forwards a few yards. I reached the door, and rang the bell. No response. Both dogs had now moved a bit closer. Perhaps they were as nervous as I was. I rang again, and tried the door. It was locked. The dogs had edged closer still, and I made a few rather pathetically friendly noises to them, hoping that they would not mistake my friendly overtures for cowardice. Another rather desperate ring on the doorbell, and the door at last opened.

'Good grief!' said my host. 'I forgot to tell you to stay in the car and hoot. I'm glad they didn't get you.'

'Yes, I'm quite glad of that too!' I said.

It's the big dogs that look the most intimidating, but I was only actually bitten by small dogs. Terriers of all kinds, and Jack Russells in particular, were the ones that got me. I was walking up the long drive to a house when I spied an Alsatian near the front door. It showed no sign of aggression, and I spoke some friendly greetings to it, at the same time keeping a wary eye on it. Suddenly, I felt a sharp pain in my calf. And there behind me was a Jack Russell, it's teeth buried in my leg. It had been hiding in the bushes at the side of the drive, and had ambushed me. I felt quite sure that it and the Alsatian had a stratagem. The Alsatian was the decoy, the Jack Russell did the ambushing. If Alsatians could laugh that Alsatian was laughing. 'Another sucker!' it said to the Jack Russell.

I was doing the first postnatal home visit to a young mother, and saw, on arrival, that she was up the garden, talking to her neighbour over the fence. I stood at the wrought iron gate, and called out a greeting.

'Hang on there, and I'll come and open the front door,' she said. As she headed for the house a small wiry terrier that had been at her side came racing down the garden towards me, barking, as I thought, in greeting. Without a pause it thrust its head through the wrought iron gate and bit me hard on the shin. It all happened in a flash. As the front door opened I realised that my trouser leg was in shreds, and blood was pouring down my leg into my shoe.

'Your dog is very friendly,' I observed, as my patient looked at the bloody scene in horror.

Of much more concern to me than my leg and trousers,

however, was that the newborn baby was lying in a carrycot on the floor, within easy reach of the dog. If it could attack me like that, what might it do to the baby which was usurping its place in the family? I gathered that I was by no means the first person it had bitten. When I called again, two days later, the dog was nowhere to be seen. Whether it had been re-homed on earth or to heaven I did not like to ask, but I sensed it was the latter.

Mrs Young rang one morning to ask for a home visit for her son, Alex, who was in bed and feeling dreadful. I said that I would call late morning.

'I shall have gone to work by then', she said, 'but my husband will be here. He works nights, and is asleep at the moment, but he will be up by the time you come.'

So it was Mr Young who answered the door when I called. We had not met before.

'Thanks for coming,' he said. 'In here,' and he showed me into the sitting room, then left, shutting the door after him. There was no sign of Alex in the room, so I assumed Mr Young had gone to fetch him. What there was in the room was a large Alsatian dog, reclining on the carpet. It showed little interest in me, and I tried to show little interest in it. I waited. The dog lay. Nobody came. It all seemed very odd. After I while I went in search of Mr Young, and found him busying himself in the kitchen.

'I'm sorry!' I said, 'I'm confused. I came to see Alex. Where is Alex?'

Mr Young gave me a long, hard, puzzled look.

'Alex!' he said. 'But Alex is at school.'

'Your wife rang this morning to say that he is ill, and in bed, and would I visit. I'm the doctor. I have come to see Alex.'

Light dawned on Mr Young's face.

'I had no idea that Alex was here at home,' he said. 'My wife had left for work by the time I woke up. I noticed that the dog was ill, and rang the vet. I thought that you were the vet. I thought you had come to see the dog.'

Perhaps doctors and vets should be more flexible, and willing to see one another's patients! It would save on home visits.

Sometimes, patients suffered injuries from their own dogs. Miss Forbes-Fortescue—the dog lady, who had dismissed me from her bedroom during my first week as a partner in the practice— called me out one Sunday afternoon. She had fallen over one of her dogs, and had pain in her chest wall. She sounded distinctly disappointed that it was me at the end of the phone. I drove to her house, made my way through the gate and past her bevy of dogs, and found her reclining uncomfortably on a settee. Deep breaths were painful. This time she allowed me to examine her. Her ribs were tender. Her breath sounds were normal.

'You have certainly bruised a couple of ribs,' I said. 'It is possible that you might have cracked one. But there is no sign of any internal damage. A rib, whether bruised or cracked, is very painful, and I will give you some pain killers to ease it.'

Miss Forbes-Fortescue looked decidedly dissatisfied.

'I b***** well want to know if it's cracked,' she protested. 'I want an x-ray.'

'Nobody will x-ray you for a painful rib,' I explained. 'Least of all on a Sunday afternoon. It's academic. The treatment is exactly the same for a bruised rib and a cracked rib. Both will mend, and the treatment is pain killers in the meantime.'

'I demand an x-ray!' said Miss Forbes-Fortescue angrily.

'I can refer you to A&E if you like,' I said. 'But it will be a wasted and painful journey. I assure you that they will not x-ray your rib. They would only do that if there was any suggestion of internal damage, but there is not.'

'If I was a b***** dog the vet would x-ray me!' she shouted, wincing at the pain.

I was trying hard, and not very successfully, to keep cool.

'What I suggest then, Miss Forbes-Fortescue, is that, when I have gone, you ring the vet and get him to see you, and arrange an x-ray for you.'

No, it was not a very satisfactory consultation, and I left feeling guilty. Miss Forbes-Fortescue moved away soon after that, and then I heard, a few years later, that she had died. Sadly, we never did become friends.

Far more dangerous to humankind than dogs were horses. I lost count of the number of patients who were injured by horses. I saw patients who had been thrown, kicked, butted, bitten, and squashed. I saw novices with saddle sores, and people with rope burns from trying to hang on to a frisky horse. Mrs James, a rather punctilious lady, decided to raise her status in the village by buying a horse. It was a rescue horse, an ancient nag that had been on its way to the knacker's yard. She kitted herself out with full, brand new riding regalia, but took the precaution of having herself and the horse led around the village, to the amusement of the villagers. At last the day came when she felt confident enough to venture out alone. Unfortunately, her nag, who had a mind of its own, walked under an apple tree, leaving Mrs James suspended, in her full riding kit, from one of the branches. As she recounted the unfortunate episode to me, in all seriousness, it was hard not to laugh. Injury to pride should be added to the list of possible mishaps from horses.

One of the most bizarre animal-inflicted injuries that I treated was that of a girl bitten through the finger by her pet lamb. She had seen her lamb, which lived in the house, chewing something. On investigation she found that it was a live electric flex. As she tried to remove it from the lamb's mouth it bit through the flex. Sparks leapt from its teeth, and she was flung one way and the lamb the other. But not before the lamb, in its spasm, bit through her finger.

Common encounters in driving around the practice were

with badgers, rabbits, squirrels, pheasants, and even the occasional stoat. On a lovely summer day my practice partner, George, was driving along a country lane in the course of his visits when he came across a pheasant, standing at the roadside. He stopped the car, thinking what a tasty meal it would make. The pheasant stood its ground. George looked around the car. A brand new golf ball lay on the back seat. He reached for it, took aim through the car window, and hurled the golf ball at the pheasant. He missed, and the pheasant flew off with loud squawks of indignation. Not wishing to lose a new golf ball George got out of the car, and, on hands and knees began to search the hedge. Just then the farmer, whose pheasant it was, happened along in his Landrover.

'Hello doctor!' he said. 'What be you looking for in that there hedge?'

Unfortunately, George never did tell us how he talked his way out of that one. Short of admitting his failed attempt at poaching, it is hard to think how he could have explained himself.

Driving to the surgery one morning I thought I had hit a squirrel. There was no sign of it in the road, and I assumed that it had avoided the car. I parked outside the surgery, and the day's work began. Some time later a receptionist, looking out at the car park, asked her colleagues, 'What is that pair of socks doing on the front of Dr Webster's car?'

They went out to investigate, and discovered a rather stunned squirrel sitting on the front bumper bar. It allowed them to pick it up. One of them took it to the local vet, who checked it over and declared it shocked but fit. The receptionist then drove it to a nearby fruit farm, and released it among the apple trees. No doubt it thought that it had arrived in heaven.

One of the saddest years, in the memory of the practice, was

2001. The Foot and Mouth disease epidemic spread across the land. Although the Prime Minister, Tony Blair, denied it, the countryside was, to all intents and purposes, closed. The hills, the fields, the riverside walks, were all closed. Farms were out of bounds. On any essential medical visits to farms, shoes and car tyres had to be disinfected. Cattle and sheep were slaughtered in their thousands. We tried to support devastated farmers, whose entire herds and flocks had been slaughtered, and who were in despair. Animals that they had reared by hand, and were known to them by name, were added to the pyres. Columns of smoke could be seen rising into the sky, where the piles of carcasses were being burned. A local road was closed for a week because the blood of culled sheep had flowed onto it. The epidemic had ripple effects into every aspect of rural life. A patient with a thriving bed and breakfast business lost £25,000 that year. Who wants to visit the countryside when it is shut down? A farmer's wife broke down in inconsolable grief, as all that they had lived for and built up seemed to have come to an end. But it was not the end. Country folk are resilient. The epidemic finally passed, the horror was over, memories faded, the tears were wiped away, and the farming community began, once again, to build up their herds and flocks. Life in the country may be idyllic in many respects. But it is also relentlessly tough. It takes tough people to live it, and it makes people tough.

ANYONE AT HOME?

One of the privileges of general practice is the access that it gives to people's homes. We enter their private realm. We see behind the respectable veneer—the smart clothes and clean socks donned for the visit to surgery. We see something of the real person. There are of course those who are as tidy at home as they are in the surgery—nothing out of place, nothing lying around. Some are minimalists, with immaculate but also sparse homes—nothing that is not strictly necessary. Few, if any, pictures hang on the walls. Mantel pieces are empty. There are certainly none of those bits and pieces of ornamental china, or souvenirs from holiday resorts, that adorn many homes, and act as receptacles for dust. No half read newspapers and magazines lying around. People with stark homes are often quite stark people—precise, efficient, matter-of-fact. At the other extreme are the chaotic ones, with houses a complete jumble—stuff everywhere, nowhere to sit, television blaring, and a scattering of snotty nosed children, or yapping dogs or scruffy cats (or all three). And, of course, lots of gaudy souvenirs stuck on shelves and walls. Most people are somewhere between these extremes. There is no right or wrong, but the state of the home speaks volumes about its occupants.

I used to find myself particularly looking out for bookshelves. The presence of books in a home in itself speaks of a person with interests beyond themselves. I would scan the books to see the sort they read—Mills and Boon or Tolstoy? Or both? My own book collection would certainly give away my interests. Home visits often turned two-dimensional patients into three-dimensional ones. It helped me to understand them better and to see them as people rather than patients.

The first challenge on any home visit was to find the right house. This was sometimes particularly difficult at night, unless it was a home I knew. Surprisingly often houses did not have their number or name clearly visible. On one particular council estate of thirty-six houses, only three had a visible, legible number. Armed with my torch I would start at one of the numbered houses and work my way round counting until I came to what I calculated to be the one I was looking for. I am surprised that I was never arrested as a burglar, particularly when I crept up close to their porches looking for some form of identification. On occasion I got it wrong. A very startled and very scantily clad young lady answered the door on one late night visit. In the background, I heard what sounded like someone trying urgently to climb into a cupboard. The damsel at the door was gratified to discover that I was not her father. Even more suspicious than creeping around porches with a torch was the occasion when an old lady whom I was visiting had lost her door key and I had to gain access by climbing through a window.

A call late one night was to a remote house down a muddy track by the river.

'Leave plenty of lights on so that I will know when I have arrived,' I said.

I found the track, and drove slowly along, looking for lights. I passed a few scattered houses in darkness, and then at last a house lit up like a cruise ship. The front door was ajar so I knocked and walked in. There were a lot of people, none of whom took the slightest notice of me. The noise of the conversations and music was deafening. The air was thick with smoke.

'Excuse me!' I shouted to one couple who appeared to be reasonably sober. 'I'm the doctor. Can you tell me who I have come to see?'

They looked at me as though they doubted my sobriety.

'The patient,' I said. 'Who is the patient I have come to see?'

The man shrugged.

'Hang on!' he said, and disappeared into the crowd.

A while later he returned with a puzzled-looking lady, obviously the hostess.

'I don't think anybody here has called you. Are you sure you are in the right house? Try the next one.'

I did, and it had a solitary outside light, glowing feebly in the dark. I knocked hesitantly in case I was wrong again. But this time it was the right house.

'I'm so glad you found us doctor. I lit up the house so that you couldn't miss it.'

'Thank you,' was all I felt able to say.

Finding the right house could be stressful if I knew that the call was urgent. It was Christmas Eve when a distraught lady rang. Her husband had collapsed. He might even be dead. Her distress was such that she could barely give me her name and address. The words tumbled incoherently from her lips. Fortunately, I knew Mr Grant well, and I knew exactly where he lived.

'Ring 999 for an ambulance,' I said, 'and I am on my way.'

I arrived some time before the ambulance, and it was to a dramatic scene. Mrs Grant was hysterical, wailing loudly. Her children were sobbing at the foot of the Christmas tree. 'Upstairs!' Mrs Grant shrieked, and I ran up them, two at a time. And there an even more dramatic scene awaited. A good-hearted neighbour—a very substantially built man, it has to be said—was administering cardiac massage with great gusto. Mr Grant was lying supine on the large double bed, and the neighbour was straddled across him, vigorously bouncing up and down on him. With every downward pressure on Mr Grant's chest the bed springs gave a groan and they both descended together. With every relaxation of pressure the bed springs sighed with relief, and they both ascended together. Mr Grant's actual chest did not appear to be being compressed one jot. It was like a dual trampoline act. Mr Grant was fortunately still able to breathe on his own, despite the weight of his rotund neighbour sitting on him. There was also no doubt that Mr Grant was in a panic, and was hyperventilating. I called for peace and calm, and, thanking the neighbour for his life-saving intentions, persuaded him to climb off Mr Grant. Gradually the panic subsided, Mr Grant's breathing began to resume a more normal pattern, and I was able to check him over. The paramedics arrived, and did their usual excellent stuff. We all concluded that Mr Grant had had a little too much Christmas fare to eat and drink, and had suffered a bout of acute indigestion. Everybody breathed a sigh of relief, and the Christmas tree lights looked particularly bright and cheerful once more.

It was not often that a home visit nearly caused a catastrophe. Mrs Jenkins, an elderly lady, had been suffering for some time from severe back pain, so I was pleased to see, on my arrival at their remote farmhouse, that she was up and about, and cooking the dinner. A smell of frying chips pervaded the house. She turned off the electric ring and showed me through to the sitting room, where Mr Jenkins was reading. I examined her, discussed her progress with them, and asked to see her tablets. Mr Jenkins said he would fetch them, but had no sooner left the room than he gave a shout: 'The kitchen is on fire!'

Instead of turning the stove off, Mrs Jenkins had accidentally turned the ring to maximum heat. The chip pan had caught fire. The kitchen was full of dense smoke and acrid fumes. Already a wooden cupboard above the stove was on fire. Polystyrene wall tiles were melting and dripping onto the stove. The plastic electric switch box above the stove was beginning to burn. I grabbed a towel, soaked it under the tap, and managed to throw it over the chip pan. Using a broom handle I was able to reach through the flames to the switch for the stove, and turn it off. Mr Jenkins and I then hurled pans of water at the burning cupboard. The smoke and fumes gradually subsided, and we (he and I, the *ad hoc* Trumpton fire brigade) were left with a scene of destruction—charred cupboard, soot-blackened walls, melted tiles, acrid fumes of burnt plastic, and, sadly, over-cooked chips. 'What a blessing you were here, doctor,' said Mrs Jenkins.

'Mrs Jenkins,' I had to point out, 'if I had not been here none of this would have happened.'

Gaining access to a patient was one thing. Getting away from them was quite another. For several years the doctors in our practice were the official police surgeons for the area. The duty doctor was liable to be called out to the local police station to examine someone under arrest, or occasionally to be called to the scene of a crime. I was asked on one occasion to attend a building site many miles away to determine whether bones that had been uncovered were human or not. On that occasion I asked that the bones be brought to me, as I was busy, and I was able to identify a very obvious jaw bone of a dog. Murder was ruled out. More usual was to attend the police station to take a blood sample from someone who had refused to be breathalysed, or to examine a possible rape victim.

On one particular occasion, the person I was asked to see had been behaving aggressively in the town, and causing a disturbance of the peace. Was he mentally ill? Did he require admission to hospital under a section of the Mental Health Act? That was my job, to decide. The police sergeant on duty was busy, with several 'customers' needing his attention. I was shown to a cell where my particular client was being held.

'I'll leave you with him to assess him,' said the sergeant. 'Ring the bell when you are finished.'

And so the door clanged shut on us both, and the key turned.

We eyed one another warily. After a few pleasantries to ease the tension I began to probe a bit more into his medical history, and it soon became apparent that he suffered from schizophrenia. He had a history of volatility and violence. It didn't take very long to conclude that it was medical attention that he needed, not imprisonment. His speech was rambling and confused, and his temper rather unpredictable, and I decided that further questioning was unnecessary, even inadvisable. I rang the bell for the sergeant. There was no sound of any bell ringing, and no response. I tried again. Nothing! I banged on the door. No response. My client began to laugh in what I imagined to be a rather maniacal way, so I reverted to chatting to distract him from my dilemma. But holding a conversation with a disturbed schizophrenic is not easy—what is there to discuss? Just as I was beginning to think that I had been forgotten the flap on the cell door opened and the sergeant peered in.

'How are you doing? Are you finished?'

'I finished some time ago. This bell doesn't work.'

'Oh no! So it doesn't. I had forgotten. I'm awfully sorry, doc.'

I did suggest as I departed that it might be wise to get it fixed before a doctor got murdered. 'Good idea!' he said.

A home visit did not always guarantee access to the home. It was a cold, foggy winter night when I was called by one of his two sisters to see old Mr Ogilvie. The three of them lived together—or so I thought—in an isolated house.

'My brother says he has got chest pain, but you never know with him,' she said, on the crackly phone.

I was surprised, on arrival, to find Mr Ogilvie lying on a hard, cold wooden bench in the dark in the garden. After a quick check to make sure that he was not on the point of death I suggested that we move him inside the house, where I could examine him more thoroughly in the light and the warmth. So I was somewhat surprised when one of his sisters replied, 'No, he doesn't come into the house. We don't let him.'

'So where does he live? Which is his room?'

'There!' she said, indicating a cold, dark shed in the garden.

'I'm sorry,' I said, 'but I must examine him in the light and in the warmth. I must insist that he comes inside the house.'

The sisters frowned and looked at one another.

'All right! Just this once!' one said grudgingly. I gathered later that the brother was a black sheep who had been exiled from the house some time previously for some unmentionable misdemeanour.

I was soon to discover that the house was little better than the shed. It was dark, cold, full of clutter, and had no running water. With such a lack of facilities, and two hostile sisters to nurse him, there was no option but to admit the old man to hospital, where, sadly, in due course, he died. Over the years, I discovered that family feuds are usually more deep-seated, more unforgiving, and more traumatic than any other kind of feud. Stubbornness and pride are often the root cause of family fall-outs. Blood is indeed thicker than water, but when it coagulates it is very difficult to get it flowing again. Occasionally, I was able to play a small part in helping relatives to learn the power of forgiveness and reconciliation.

The sorts of home visit that I dreaded most were those involving mental illness. It was not because of the nature of the illness as such, but because of the time that these visits often took. If there was any question of the patient needing immediate psychiatric assessment, or of needing admission to hospital under a section of the Mental Health Act, I knew that I would be there for a considerable time, and all other work had to go on hold.

Roger was a man with long-term mental health problems, and was cared for by his elderly father. From time to time a crisis would arise, and I got involved in one such crisis. He had been increasingly restless and confused, pacing endlessly round the garden and refusing to enter the house. Finally, he fell, and cut his head. That was when his long-suffering father at last called for help. Roger and I had a mobile consultation, walking round and round a compost heap. He clearly needed hospital admission and further assessment, but was completely unable to accept this. As we talked and walked he constantly picked at his cut head, spreading blood to hands, face and clothing. Admission by section was going to be necessary, and that meant calling out a psychiatrist and a social worker. I groaned inwardly. While waiting for their arrival it seemed opportune to stitch Roger's cut head. It would be one thing less to do at hospital. With the assistance of a burly neighbour I did my suturing, whereupon Roger resumed his restless pacing of the large garden. I followed a few paces behind, to ensure that he did not undo my stitch work.

At last a small van drew into the drive. It contained several yapping dogs and a rather jolly, mini-skirted psychiatrist. She disappeared into the house. I went to find a neighbour who could take my place watching Roger, as he paced round and round the garden. By the time I was able to join the psychiatrist and Roger's father in the house, much of the necessary paperwork had already been filled in. But it soon became apparent that the psychiatrist had assumed that Roger's father was the patient, and, puzzled as to why it was needed, he had obediently furnished details of his own name and medical history. The father was saved in the nick of time from being consigned to a mental health ward, and we began the process again. The correct patient, Roger, was eventually conveyed to a place of safety and care, and the exhausted father was able to enjoy a brief period of respite. Let us never underestimate the toll taken by those who care for sick relatives, often long term, and sometimes with very little back-up support.

COPING WITH PROGRESS

It was the early hours of the morning. I had been called to the home, on a housing estate, of someone with acute abdominal pain. Having established that it was no more than acute indigestion I was just walking out of their front door when my mobile phone rang. It was my wife, Rosemary, to tell me that there had been another call. When she gave me the address I thought she must be confusing it with the call that I had just done. It was the very next door house! With houses on modern estates being built very close together, I only had to take a couple of steps sideways, and I was ringing their doorbell. The lady who answered had a look of utter astonishment.

'Doctor!' she gasped. 'But I have literally only just put the phone down, after speaking to your wife! How on earth did you get here so quickly?'

I shrugged nonchalantly.

'We tend to hang around on people's doorsteps at night, just in case,' I said. 'It's all part of the service!'

She gave me a funny look, totally puzzled by my instant appearance. It was the beginning of the mobile phone era. Reception was not yet reliable enough for calls to be routed direct to the mobile phone, but it meant that our receptionists during the day, and our spouses at night, could get in touch with us quickly. To be called to adjacent houses in the middle of the night was, however, most unusual.

The advent of mobile phones transformed our on-call lives. I was reminded of a story told me by an elderly lady, Eva. She had grown up at the foot of the hills in the days before the advent of even the landline telephone—at least, before its advent in rural areas. When she was about eight years old her little sister became acutely ill. She developed a high temperature, a raging sore throat, and difficulty breathing. Was it the dreaded diphtheria? It was night time, and the doctor lived in the village five miles away. The only way to call him was to go on foot. So Eva was sent by her mother. She ran, barefoot, in the dark, all the way to the village, and roused the doctor from his bed. But when he heard the symptoms he said that it was almost certainly diphtheria, that there was nothing he could do, that there was no point in him getting out his horse and carriage, and to let him know in the morning if she was still alive. He gave Eva advice as to their care of her sister, and he went back to bed. She ran all the way home. By morning her sister was indeed dead. How life must have been transformed by the advent of the telephone, and by the motorcar.

In my early days in the practice we had landline telephones, but mobiles had yet to be born. When going out on calls, whether from home or surgery, I had to leave an itinerary of my intended visits.

'I plan to visit Mrs X first—she sounds quite poorly. She is on the phone—her number will be in the directory. Then on to Mr Y at Pound Close. He doesn't have a phone, but his neighbour, Mrs Z, does. Her number is ——' And so we mapped out our proposed route for home visits. Quite often we were met, at people's homes, with the words, 'The surgery/your wife rang, doctor. Can you ring them back. It sounded quite urgent. Here's the phone.' And so messages got passed on, the ringer trying to keep a step ahead of wherever we had got to in our visits.

Then came the pager—a simple little device which had two rings—a rapid beep for urgent and a slower beep for non-urgent. If the rapid beep went off we would hurry to our next visit in order to use their phone, or pull in at the nearest house and ask to use theirs, or look out for the nearest phone box. It saved our receptionists or spouses from ringing around the countryside to find us.

The memorable day came when our very first mobile phone was delivered to the surgery. There was just the one, to be carried by the doctor on call. It was the size, shape and weight of a brick, but, unlike a brick, it was also graced with a great stalk of an aerial, a rigid prong, projecting from its top. Dialling was done on an array of buttons down one side of the brick. The phone required the exclusive use of one hand to carry it, leaving the other hand free for everything else— medical case, patient's notes, and any bottles of medicine or tablets that we might be carrying. We were inordinately proud of this state-of-the-art device, and its cumbersomeness was outweighed by its usefulness.

Gradually each generation of mobile phone was replaced by another, smaller and smaller, increasingly sleek and progressively clever. The day came when we were each presented with our own individual mobile. But somehow these slim, pocket-friendly, modest but clever little machines never had quite the same presence as the brick, which ended its days lying in state in the doctors' coffee room, its prong projecting as proudly as ever.

A seminal day in the life of the practice was 18 September 1990. The first computers arrived. Life would never be the same again. The multi-user system cost £28,000, and I had extreme doubts as to the justification for this expense. Technology (of any kind) and I have never been the best of friends, and I regarded the spanking new VDU reposing on my desk with great suspicion. It gazed at me with similar mistrust.

'What on earth am I supposed to do with this?' I thought to myself.

Having ignored it for a week I tentatively put finger to keyboard for the first time, expecting it either to bite, or to erase everything on its memory (which, at that stage, wasn't much). A wary friendship began to develop—very wary, very gradual. Entries and observations made on the computer seemed so impersonal. The old, hand-written records, entered on cards and kept in a 'Lloyd-George' envelope (perversely, blue for a lady and red for a man), were somehow personal, both to the patient and to the doctor. Some patients had fat, well-worn envelopes, fraying at the edges and crammed with medical history. For others the envelopes were slim and good as new after many years, and contained almost no records at all. One glance at the envelope spoke volumes. The notes of some patients were singed and blackened—the legacy of a fire some years previously at the home of one of the village doctors. It was obvious too, from the handwriting, which doctor had last seen the patient. What they had actually written about that consultation might not be so obvious—particularly if the last doctor to see them had been my partner George. His handwriting was notoriously difficult to decipher, but it did ensure total confidentiality! Even he sometimes could not decipher his own minute spidery scrawl. The new, computer records were at least very legible, but they seemed somehow soulless, and lacking in any personal touch. But, little by little I was won over, a most reluctant convert.

Computers and mobile phones transformed general practice more than any other innovations. They were tools to be used, and over which we had some control. We had to make sure, however, that we did control them, and that they did not control us. There was, and is, always the danger of technological communication replacing human contact; of the doctor's focus being on machine rather than patient. The caricature arose of the computerised GP, eyes glued to his computer screen, tapping furiously at his keyboard, while the patient sits to one side, passively answering questions, but with no eye contact with the doctor. It was so easy to allow the computer to come between us, and I had consciously to swivel my chair to face the patient, establish eye contact, and to listen. Computer entries came ideally after the patient had left.

A huge advantage that computers brought was the ability to record and to retrieve data. Blood pressure measurements, weight, alcohol consumption, smoking habits, immunisations, blood test results and so on could all now be recorded, and the information retrieved and compared readily. This was a goldmine of health and sociological data. Rightly the authorities encouraged doctors to record these facts for every patient. But simple encouragement is not always enough. Sometimes there has to be a financial carrot. A reward of some sort. And so QOF (Quality Outcomes Framework) points were introduced. GPs were rewarded according to the number of their patients who had had their data recorded. This was fine, and for our practice proved very satisfactory. We were soon scoring nearly 100 per cent on our QOF points. The danger comes when the recording of data becomes the main objective, from the doctor's point of view, of the consultation.

A possible scenario arose: Mr X might be extremely worried about a certain symptom. He goes to his GP. The GP, eyes glued to his computer screen, is only half listening as Mr X explains his worries. The doctor is actually checking to see if any QOF-relevant records need to be updated. Mr X comes to the end of his soliloquy.

'So, what do you think doctor?'

'Oh, I don't think you've got anything to worry about Mr X,' replies the doctor rather vaguely.

'By the way, I see we haven't checked your blood pressure for a while, so let me just do that while you are here.' And Mr

X goes away feeling that his worries haven't really been listened to. That scenario is an exaggeration, but it is also a potential danger.

As well as the advent of mobile phones and computers, the advance of medical technology has profoundly affected the way medicine is practised—and has also affected the cost of delivering medical care. In my early days of practise the available technology was limited to some basic blood tests, and X-rays, and an ECG. Accurate diagnosis depended very much on a detailed history, and then thorough and systematic physical examination. You used hands and eyes and ears. You listened for crepitations and rubs and murmurs and clicks and borborygmi. You percussed for resonance and shifting dullness. You felt for lumps and spleen tips and abdominal splash. You elicited reflexes and assessed muscle tone. You made and recorded careful clinical observations. Then, and only then, you ordered tests, if confirmation of your findings was needed. Two things have tended to change all that. First is the advent and availability of all kinds of tests -fast routes to diagnosis. There are all kinds of clever ways of imaging, with scans and radio-isotopes. There is a plethora of blood tests, and genetic analysis. The temptation is to rush to tests before doing a thorough clinical assessment. Second is the advent of American-style medical litigation, with the inevitable consequence of defensive medicine—a fear of being accused of not having investigated a patient sufficiently, or of having missed a diagnosis. So highly expensive investigations may be done 'just to be sure'. Of course, progress is to be welcomed with open hands, but not at the expense of good, old-fashioned, time-consuming open-eared, hands-on clinical medicine.

Much of the progress in medicine is not actually due to technology. It's to do with the way professionals work together. It's to do with good communication. Thanks to my energetic and forward-thinking partners our practice was always innovative.

We didn't wait for change to happen to us—we often took the initiative. We were among the very first practices to introduce attached health visitors, attached physiotherapists, and, in 1992, an attached social worker. Sadly, GPs and social workers had, in many instances, become hostile to, and suspicious of, one another. They often seemed to be working against one another, to the detriment of patient care. By incorporating an attached social worker into the practice team we became friends, not enemies; we communicated on a daily basis; we defined our priorities, goals and strategies together, shared information, and cooperated at every level. In 1995 I became GP representative on a working party to assess and advise on the care of the elderly mentally ill. We had by then already appointed an attached health visitor with the specific role of assessing and providing for the needs of the elderly. Our model for communication, respite care, and other services was adopted by the Working Party. It was gratifying to be at the forefront of innovations that really made a difference to patient care.

Central to our Primary Care team success was our monthly practice lunch. The whole Primary Care team— doctors, practice manager, practice nurses, district nurses, health visitors, midwives, physiotherapists, social workers, school nurse, chiropodist, receptionists—even, for a while, the vicar—met in our waiting room, and had a buffet lunch provided by the practice. We usually began with a speaker, and then, without breaking confidences, shared information and concerns. There were usually about thirty of us. We gelled as a team, and found ourselves playing together for the same side— the side of our patients. It was a model that was adopted by many other practices. In 1999 the practice won two National Beacon awards—one for our Attached Social Worker project, and one for our Time-4-U School Clinics (spear-headed by our newest partner, Andy).

All this was encouraging and gratifying. The question,

though, remained—how do you really measure good patient care? Is it by ticking boxes of measurable data? This may give an indication of success, but it gives only part of the story. You cannot easily measure and quantify compassion, care, kindness, and the quality of listening. This is best assessed by the honest feedback from patients, and by and large that was very reassuring. I visited an elderly lady who was dying. It was her eighty-eighth birthday, so I took her a single rose from our garden—a small gesture for her last birthday. A few days later I visited again. The rose, now withered, was still at her bedside.

'Shall I throw this out for you?' I asked.

'No! Leave it!' she said. 'It was my only birthday present. Thank you!' And she gave me a kiss. That was better than any QOF point or Beacon award.

FINDING A PARTNER

There are some words in the English language whose meaning has changed—or at least which can now be understood in more than one way. 'Gay' and 'cool' are two such. The word 'gay' can never now be used as a synonym for 'happy' or 'carefree'. Likewise, something that is exciting and heart-warming and trendy might be described by the modern generation as being, not 'warm', but 'cool'. Another such word is 'partner'. A professional or a businessman who works with colleagues must beware of such sentences as 'May I introduce my partner, Jenny, to you?' This could be quite misunderstood, and could give rise to a complete misconception about their relationship. So when I speak of 'finding a partner' I am referring to the professional variety. For advice on finding the other kind of partner look elsewhere!

I was invited to join the practice, as a partner, half way through my year as trainee. By then we had all got to know each other well. We understood how each of us ticked. We knew whether or not we would have a good and happy working relationship. I am sure that I was not the best on the market, but at least I was a known quantity. 'Better the devil that you know . . .' Likewise, when we expanded the practice, and appointed Sue, she was our trainee. She knew us, we knew her. We knew the person we were getting, and we liked what we knew—which is why she was appointed.

However, when appointing our next partner, we decided to look at a wider field of candidates, and to advertise. The response was overwhelming. Seventy-five applicants wrote in. How were we to shortlist, and then make a final choice? Clearly the first things to look at were training, qualifications, and medical experience. But they proved to be no help at all. Almost all had qualified at reputable medical schools and done amazing things during their 'elective periods' as students. All had good degrees. Most had gained useful experience in their hospital internships, or 'house jobs'. All had worked for at least a year in general practice. Most had gone on to acquire Membership of the Royal College of General Practitioners, the specialising examination for GPs. Most had excellent references. How were we to choose a short list from all of them? We searched the applications for clues about character and initiative—for something that made a candidate stand out from the rest.

One possible candidate, Julian, had been a doctor in the army, posted to Afghanistan. He had been working with special forces, under very challenging conditions. That stood out for us. But some other candidates had also done impressive things. We selected a short list, including Julian, and invited them for interview. It was a Sunday, a few days before the interviews. George was the partner on call. When he drove into the surgery, to collect some medication for a patient, he found a very smart little open-topped sports car in the car park. Sitting in the passenger seat was a very attractive young lady. There was no sign of the driver.

'Can I help you?' asked George. 'Were you looking for a doctor?'

The young lady looked embarrassed, and glanced towards the high wall that surrounded the surgery garden.

'Um, well, actually, to be honest, my fiance was just taking a look around,' she said.

Just then there was a squeak, and the door to the garden

opened, having been unbolted from the other side. A handsome young man emerged, a bit scruffy from having scaled the wall to get into the garden. He looked a bit taken aback to have been caught red-handed, trespassing in the surgery garden.

'I'm Julian,' he said. 'I have applied to join the practice, and am coming for interview next week. I hope you don't mind but I wanted to have a look at the premises before coming for interview—just to get the feel of the place.'

We had been looking for someone with that extra bit of character. To us a bit of thorough military-style surveillance showed initiative and real enthusiasm for the job. Our feelings were confirmed at interview, and Julian joined us as our new partner. As far as I am aware he has never had to abseil into a patient's flat, or blow open their front door with a controlled explosion, but his military background brought to the practice thoroughness and efficiency which greatly benefited us.

The standards we looked for in appointing our practice manager and nurses were no less demanding than for a partner—though I don't recall any prospective nurse scaling the garden wall. We wanted a team of excellence. It takes only one rotten potato to ruin the mash. We were fortunate in having an excellent and committed team throughout. It might be thought that the choice of receptionists requires less stringent standards than for the medical staff, but not so. The receptionist is the front line of the practice. She (or he) is the shop window. They, more than anyone, give the practice its character and its reputation.

All too often doctors' receptionists are described as 'dragons', past whom it is very difficult to get. They wield power, and can have the say as to whether or not you get to see a doctor. When a receptionist does have dragon-like qualities (and thankfully none of ours ever did) I ask myself 'Who is it that allows, or possibly even encourages, the receptionist to behave like this?' And the answer has to be 'The doctor.' Some doctors cultivate dragons so that they can hide behind them, and be protected by them. There is nothing more galling than to fight one's way past a dragon only to find a charming St George of a doctor, who gives every appearance of having no idea of the battle it took to get there. Of course they know! Or, if they don't they should make it their business to.

Most of the time receptionists are dealing with people who want routine appointments for routine problems. But who is to know what lies behind the request for an appointment? Fear, anxiety, stress, depression? The good receptionist is sensitive to the moods and attitudes of patients, and is tolerant and understanding when people are brusque. There are, however, a minority of patients who are just plain rude, and unreasonably demanding. These soon become known, and the good receptionist has to exercise all her powers of patience and firmness.

For many years, during 'out of hours' times (nights, weekends) it was the doctors' wives or husbands who took the calls, when the partner on call was already out on a visit. We were all blessed with wonderful wives and husbands, who knew how to reassure and calm people, and to advise what to do in emergencies. They got to know, by voice, some of our frequent callers. On many occasions I was asked by patients to thank my wife for 'being so kind and helpful' when she had taken an out of hours phone call.

I am married to a walking telephone directory, and her phenomenal memory for phone numbers was useful on many an occasion. Except one! A distraught lady rang in the middle of the night to say that her husband, a patient of my partner, David, had collapsed. She was so distraught that she couldn't explain to me where she lived. She was shrieking down the phone.

'Please come quickly!'

'I'm on my way!' I said

By now my wife was wide awake.

'I'll have to ring David and ask for directions,' I said. 'What's his home number?'

My resident telephone directory rattled off the number with confidence, and I dialled it.

The phone rang and rang.

'That's odd,' I thought. 'Either he hasn't got a phone next to his bed, or he is very sound asleep.'

Finally, as I was desperately wondering what to do, a very sleepy and grumpy voice answered. It wasn't David. Rosemary had mistakenly given me the number of friends whose bedroom was three floors above their telephone in the hall.

'I'm very sorry! Wrong number!' I said, and put the phone down on some very colourful language. I don't think that, to this day, they know that it was I who rang—unless they read this! The outcome on that occasion was a happy one. A hypoglycaemic coma (a low blood sugar level in a man with diabetes) was soon remedied with an injection of glucose.

In the days before we employed a practice nurse it fell to the receptionists to do some of the routine urine testing. Sometimes I was asked to show a new receptionist how to test urine for sugar. This provided a good opportunity for some fun. I would dip my finger in the sample, and then lick the finger, tasting it carefully to assess the sugar level. The new receptionist's face would meanwhile be a picture of disgust, and regret at ever having applied for the job. Of course, needless to say, I had swapped fingers! When I discovered that one new member of staff had been forewarned about me by her colleagues I swapped the genuine specimen for a sample of grape juice, which looked remarkably like urine. Instead of dipping my finger in the sample, I took a sip, and, smacking my lips, declared the patient to be free of diabetes. Her disbelief and horror were relieved when I assured her that she could, if she preferred, use a urine testing stick.

As the practice grew, and in spite of three extensions, we again began to outgrow our facilities and space. General practice had become so much more complex. We now

employed so many more staff. It was time for a completely
new building, on a new site. Step by step we moved towards
this goal—acquiring land and planning consent. It was vitally
important that the new building would provide enough space
for everyone, and be designed in an attractive but efficient
way. It must meet, not only present requirements, but future
needs. A memorable day was when we all had an 'away day' at
a local hotel. Everybody—doctors, practice manager, cleaners,
nurses, handyman, receptionists, health visitors, midwives,
physiotherapists, the local dental practice, pharmacy staff,
gardener, podiatrist, everybody who worked in any way at the
surgery, and representatives of patients and Community Care—
all had an opportunity for blue-sky thinking, and to present
their wish-list. The ideas of that day were then incorporated
into the new surgery by the architects.

I never worked in the spanking new surgery. My retirement
was due, and it seemed right for my successor to be in the new
building from the beginning. But on the day of the Grand
Opening I did have the privilege of introducing royalty to
retired members of the surgery team. I now have the occasional
pleasure of sitting in the bright new reception area, and taking
my turn along with everyone else—and feeling proud and
content that the legacy of excellence continues.

PHYSICIAN, HEAL THYSELF

Doctors don't get sick. Or at least they are not supposed to. They are there to diagnose and treat and support you in your time of need. There is no time for them to be ill. I had been blessed with good health. Apart from adventures with malaria and infectious hepatitis as a child in Kenya, and the regulatory mumps and measles, I had enjoyed good health. When dealing with patients I tried to put myself into their shoes. What must their constant pain be like? How hopeless does one feel in a deep depression? What is it like to face the prospect of death? I tried to empathise. But empathy, however well meant, can never be the same as the real experience.

My problem really began shortly before we were due to fly to Australia to visit family. It was a twitching of my muscles—what doctors call fasciculation. It affected my legs, insteps, arms and hands. I felt it more than saw it, and took little notice. A few days previously I had applied weed killer in a rather casual and careless way to a large patch of nettles. The herbicide had got onto my arms and had soaked my trouser legs. Silly me! Probably it was an effect of that. I ignored the twitches, and we flew off to Australia.

Our son and family lived in Darwin, in the far north of Australia, and had gone there to work among the Aborigine population. On our arrival they told us excitedly that we had all been invited by Aborigine friends to visit their home on the remote, wild, sparsely populated Cobourg Peninsular. This was Aborigine territory, closed to outsiders except by the invitation and permission of Aborigine residents. The invitation to us was a huge privilege, and we all looked forward to the visit with excitement. It was excitement laced, however, with apprehension. To enter the Cobourg we had to cross the East Alligator River. The crossing was by causeway—there was no bridge.

Paul's Aborigine friends continued: 'The river is tidal there, although quite a long way inland. When the tide is in it is too deep to cross. When the tide is going out the current is strong, and it can turn your car. So point it slightly upstream as you cross. If possible time your crossing for exactly two hours after low tide at the coast. If you are unfortunately swept off the causeway, whatever you do stay in your car—the river is teeming with salt-water crocodiles who will get you.'

Very reassuring advice! We checked carefully on coastal tide times, and headed for the Kakadu National Park, our jumping off point for the Cobourg Peninsular.

The next day, our arrival at the East Alligator River crossing was timed with obsessional exactitude. We drove down the approach to the crossing. How deep would the water be, and how swift the current? We were greeted by the sight of a totally exposed causeway, and a line of children happily fishing from it. Our somewhat hysterical laughter was that of relief, mingled with a sense of having been fooled. But then we observed the muddy river banks, and the very high tide marks, and we knew that the advice had been sincerely meant. We entered the Cobourg Peninsular with a sense of adventure.

Having got the dreaded river crossing behind us, we decided to stop for a break. An outcrop of rocks, and some shady trees, seemed an ideal picnic spot. Paul wandered off towards the rocky cliff to relieve himself, and a few minutes later called out: 'Dad! Would you recognise human bones if you saw them?'

'I certainly hope so,' I replied, thinking of years of anatomy study and surgery.

'Come and look at these.'

He was standing at the entrance to a cave. We entered, and there, littering the ground, were hundreds of human bones. Skulls, femurs, ribs. They jostled randomly with one another. They were not intact skeletons, and it looked as though they might have been dragged about by wild animals. It was an ossuary, but one provided by nature. It reminded me of Ezekiel's vision of the valley of dry bones. We realised very quickly that we were standing on sacred Aborigine ground, and we beat a hasty retreat. We had intruded where we should not have been.

Feeling somewhat guilty of our intrusion, we continued our journey. Our travel instructions seemed rather vague.

'You will pass through a swampy bit. Take a left turn there, then exactly fifteen kilometres after that you will see a rough track turning off to the right. Follow that to the edge of the sea, and it will bring you to our house.'

And so, after bumping through a mile or more of scrub, and circumnavigating fallen trees, we came to a wonderful expanse of sandy beach, shaded by clumps of casuarinas. Waves were pounding the shore, and the blue sea and surf were begging us to plunge in and cool ourselves. The heat was intense. Our friends soon appeared, and gave us a royal welcome. Their house stood back a bit from the beach—a simple, homely building, knocked together, with basic facilities. The shower was a tap under a rainwater tank. The toilet was a little corrugated iron hut perched above a forty-gallon drum containing lime. A modicum of privacy was afforded by some hessian sacking draped across the front of the hut. It was easy to tell if the toilet was occupied—you could see the occupant's legs. But the basic conditions were more than made up for by the warmth of our welcome. We were invited to pitch our small two-man tents on the beach.

Our visions of wallowing in the warm sea were soon dispelled.

'The sea is full of crocodiles. It is not safe to enter the water. You can see their footprints in many places, where they have come up the beach at night to lie in wait for wild pigs.'

Our hosts indicated a small, thickly vegetated billabong a few hundred yards inland.

'The pigs come there to eat the fruits of the bushes, and the crocodiles ambush them,' our hosts explained.

'At night light a fire on the beach between your tents and the sea, and don't let it go out. Stoke it throughout the night.'

We only needed telling once. We set about collecting a stack of driftwood, and, sure enough, as we walked up the beach we saw fresh tracks of crocodiles leading up the beach towards the billabong. What concerned me was that we didn't see any tracks leading back to the sea, suggesting that the crocodiles were still at the billabong. I hoped that they would not choose that moment to return, as we were passing. A crocodile can outrun a man.

That night we sat with our hosts round a camp fire on the beach, eating turtle eggs that they had harvested earlier— taking just two or three from a nest, and carefully re-covering the rest. Raphael and Maria told us tales of the bush, and recounted Aborigine folk legends.

'Soon after you entered The Cobourg' said Raphael, his dark bearded face lit up by the flickering fire, 'you passed a place that is very sacred to us. There is a cave, where we lay our dead with their ancestors.'

Paul and I glanced at one another, but we did our best to look surprised at this information. We dare not tell Raphael what we had done and seen.

'My father's body was laid there, and his bones rest there, but his spirit now lives here in the sea. You may notice a very large crocodile that swims up and down just off the shore.

That is my father's spirit. It is him, watching over his ancestral land.'

The thought crossed my mind that it might be quite consoling to be eaten by a crocodile knowing that it was Raphael's dad! But on second thoughts I was not very keen to meet him.

With our stomachs full of bush tucker, and our minds full of Aborigine tales, we crawled late that night into our flimsy mosquito net domes in the sand. We had stoked the fire up well, and had a plentiful supply of wood. But the thought of crocodiles was not far from our minds. I was just dropping off to sleep when there was a sudden scrabbling noise a few feet away. I grabbed my torch, and there, passing our tent was what looked like a crocodile—except that it was too small.

It was a monitor lizard, about three feet long, which, as we discovered next morning, lived nearby and regularly visited the area in search of food scraps. Sleep was fitful that night, and on the following nights. And as I lay, half awake, ears listening for the sound of reptilian footsteps, and one eye on the fire, I became more aware than ever of a constant twitching of the muscles in my arms and legs.

Those fitful nights gave me plenty of time to think, and thinking at night is not always a good thing. The imagination can run away. Things seem worse than they do by the light of day. And my mind turned to one of the things that I, as a doctor, dreaded most. Motor Neurone Disease. MND.

I had had several patients die of this dreadful condition. I had watched them gradually deteriorate. It was top of my list of illnesses that I would most hate to have. And one of the main signs of MND is fasciculation of the muscles. As I lay in our hot little mosquito dome, and dwelled on this fact, I became more and more convinced that that was what I had. What else could explain my symptoms?

I said nothing about my fears to the family—it was too precious a time together to spoil it with my anxieties. But the thought, the dread, of MND was constantly on my mind. As we walked along the wild beach, with its crocodile footprints and crashing waves, I began to feel—or was it to imagine?—that my legs were a bit heavy; that I was tending to drag them a bit in the soft sand.

I began to long to get home to England, to get this sorted out. The day after we got home I told Rosemary of my fears, and was immediately enveloped in love and prayer. I then went to consult George. He rightly felt that his examination couldn't provide any clear diagnosis either way, and he arranged an early appointment for neurophysiological tests. I had wires connected up to me, and needles thrust into me, including into the base of my tongue. It was a new experience to be at the receiving end of medical procedures. The results were quite reassuring, but not diagnostic, so the next stop was to see a local neurologist. He was thorough in his examination, and quite matter-of-fact in his manner. No, he did not think I had MND, but he could not explain the fasciculations that I was experiencing. I should go away and forget them, and get on with life.

I was initially greatly reassured. He did not 'think' that I had MND. The busy, day-to-day life of general practice took over. But the twitching continued, and by then I had become very conscious of it, and introspective about it. How often had I gently admonished patients for being too introspective? The initial reassurance that I had felt began to dissipate. What was going on? Something must be causing the symptoms. Or was I imagining them? Family and friends and my partners in the practice were hugely supportive. Above all Rosemary's love and patience with me, and her prayers, kept me going. I found it increasingly difficult to pray myself—my own spiritual life was overwhelmed by my anxiety. I relied on the prayers of others, and the loving prayer ministry and anointing that I received from our church leaders. I was an emotional and spiritual cripple, leaning heavily on others.

The weeks and months passed. I tried not to let my own problems intrude on my treatment of patients, but by the end of the day I was spent, wrung out. My legs felt heavy, I could see no future, felt no hope, had problems sleeping, woke early each morning dreading another day. And only then did it dawn on me—what Rosemary had already perceived—that my real problem now was not the muscle twitching. It was clinical depression that had crept up on me as a result of my anxieties. If I had been one of my own patients I would have seen it coming. Now, for the first time, I knew what it was like to see nothing but blackness. To live in a void of despair. I was started on antidepressant treatment, and referred back to the neurologist for review. With an audible sigh, and a sense of his exasperation, he referred me on to a consultant at the regional hospital, an authority on MND. I saw her three months later. She was brilliant, with that gift that all doctors should strive for, of listening in such a way that makes you feel that they are there for nobody but you. She was totally reassuring. In the previous two years she had seen twenty-seven patients with unexplained fasciculations, and seven of them were doctors. We probably know too much for our own good, and worry about things that others would ignore. My appointment with her was a turning point.

Three months later I felt well enough to go on a sailing holiday in Croatia with our daughter and her husband. I was assured that, apart from hauling on a few ropes, it would not be too physically demanding. And so it was that we came to be moored in the little harbour of Stari Grad, on the island of Hvar. Behind the harbour was a steep hill, and at the top of the hill a stone cross. Somewhat on the spur of the moment, Rosemary and I decided to climb up to the cross. We passed quaint old houses, then up a steep path through pine woods. The views over Hvar were wonderful. And so we arrived at the cross—a cross erected by a man in thanks to God for saving his life. As we sat resting at the foot of the cross it suddenly occurred to me that I had climbed a steep hill without needing to rest—something that I had not been able to do for a long time. And I had had no muscle twitching for a while. My legs felt normal. I had already made a decision that morning to phase out the antidepressants. As I sat on that hilltop, at the foot of that cross, an overwhelming feeling came that my healing was complete. It was a year, almost to the day, since it had all begun. It had been a long and painful journey, and I had learned a lot. Once I knew all about anxiety, depression, fear. Now I didn't just know about it—I knew it; I had been there. I had been reminded that medicine does not always have nice, clear-cut explanations and answers—it is as much an art as a science. Nobody had been able to explain my symptoms. They had told me what they were not, but not what they were. It was a reminder that life is full of mysteries. I had learned the power of the mind over the body, and of the body over the mind—they are inseparable. I had also learned the power of love and of prayer.

That evening, back on the boat, our daily Bible reading happened to be Psalm 30.

'O Lord my God, I cried to You for help, and You have healed me . . . You have restored me to life. You have clothed me with joy . . . O Lord my God, I will give thanks to You for ever.'

THE ART OF RE-TYRING

The mystery of my twitching muscles never was resolved. Was it weed-killer? Was it a benign form of fasciculation? Had I imagined it all? What was certain was that, after a year, it all settled down. But the depression that had come with it, or as a result of it, probably had another, background contributory factor—I was coming up to the age of retirement, and I dreaded it. My ambition, from the age of four, had been to be a doctor. My whole working life had been taken up by doctoring. Whether as an exhausted houseman, working or on-call for over one hundred hours a week; or whether rummaging in someone's abdomen by the light of a hurricane lamp in the depths of the African bush; or whether setting out on the third or fourth night call on a bitter winter's night, I had never regretted my vocation. Putting aside the red tape, and the constantly changing administrative structure of the NHS, I loved my work. Working with good colleagues, and making a difference for patients, was all I asked. But without a doubt medicine had been all-consuming. There had been a price to pay in terms of family life, and social life; of hobbies and recreation. Fortunately I had been blessed with an understanding wife and family, who accepted that often work had to come first; that medicine was not a job but a vocation. Life in retirement was going to be very different. Inevitably, and relentlessly, the day of retirement came. We had a wonderful party with all the practice staff, past and present, and their spouses and children. Next morning I woke with the feeling of having been stripped bare of my purpose in life.

What was it that I missed? I asked myself in the weeks and months ahead. It was the camaraderie of the surgery. It was my patients, many of whom I regarded as friends. But, more than that, it was the loss of significance. As a doctor you play a key role in other people's lives. You share confidential information. You give advice. You encourage and comfort. You can make a difference for others in all sorts of ways—even sometimes the difference between life and death. Suddenly all that is gone. The General Medical Council makes it very clear that you are now a has-been. You are told that you must, under no circumstances, act as a doctor, or give the impression that you are a doctor. You must not diagnose or treat, and cannot any longer write prescriptions—not even private prescriptions for your own family. At one point the GMC even wanted to stop retired doctors from using the title 'Doctor'. One felt like an army officer who has been stripped of all their insignia, and reduced to the ranks.

I feel for doctors who retire, and who have no other interests in life—those for whom the practice of medicine has been absolutely everything, all-consuming, and they are left with nothing. That can be a death sentence. I was fortunate. I was very involved in church activities. I had a large garden to occupy me. I had other roles in life, and plenty to do. But I still missed my medical work. It was about a year to the day since retirement when I was driving to our daughter's house. The sun was shining. I had a useful job to do—I was going to repair her garage roof. All was well in the world, and for the first time I felt really positive about retirement. It was actually good to have time to do other things.

The first job on the garage roof was to bolt some cross

beams in place. It was a high roof, and I needed a long ladder. Drill, bolt. Drill, bolt. It was going well. Then I realised that I had left the drill resting on the previous beam. I leaned across to get it—and the next thing I knew I was landing on the concrete floor, on my side, with a crump. My head had narrowly missed the waiting stack of beams. I lay for a bit, gathering my thoughts. I must get up. But I couldn't get up. This was ridiculous, I thought. If I sat up all would become normal and well. But as I tried to sit up I heard as much as felt a loud crunch in my left hip area. I realised that my foot was facing in a very odd direction. Clearly my femur was broken.

There was nobody around. It was an isolated house. But, fortuitously, and only because Rosemary had insisted, I had a mobile phone in my pocket. I knew that she was counselling someone that morning, and was not surprised to find both our home phone and her mobile on answerphone. I tried to ring several times, but then dialled 999 myself. Before long I heard the siren of an ambulance. It passed the end of the road twice. They couldn't find me. Then Rosemary rang me—she had sensed from the repeated calls that something was wrong. Suddenly it seemed everybody was there at once—paramedics, wife, her counselling client, daughter. In my helplessness I was so glad to see them all, and to surrender myself to the paramedics' expert care. Morphine and entonox brought relief, but the greatest relief was to feel in safe hands. I was the patient, not the doctor.

They couldn't operate that day, and I shared a ward with three elderly patients, all awaiting hip replacements. As I lay with my leg, badly fractured in three places, in a splint, I hoped that my three companions would not discover that I was a doctor. Unfortunately one of them asked the nurse a medical question which she could not answer, and she said to him: 'He's the one you need to ask. He's a doctor.'

My anonymity was blown, and all three began to question

me eagerly about their medical problems. I thought of the
GMC advice—do not even give the impression that you are a
doctor. What was I to do?

'Look,' I said, trying to sound reasonable. 'I am not on duty
at the moment, and my leg is pretty sore. I will answer one
question each, then I shall go to sleep.'

So Question Time followed, one each, and then I closed
down.

I had been pondering who would do my operation the next
day. I knew all the orthopaedic surgeons. Would it be the hip
and leg specialist? I hoped so—I trusted him. And who would
give me my anaesthetic? I so hoped it would be a particular
senior anaesthetist, whom I liked and respected very much.
Next morning the anaesthetist came to check me—but not my
favourite. In fact he seemed barely old enough to be out of
school.

'I'm going to give you a spinal anaesthetic,' he said. I
understood why. I had done hundreds of operations in Africa
under spinal anaesthetic, and it gave excellent relaxation of the
muscles. But . . .

'The only thing is,' I told him 'My leg is so painful and
unstable that I don't think I could possibly turn on my side or
sit up for you to inject the spinal.'

'I tell you what,' he said brightly. 'I'll knock you out for a
few minutes with ketamine, and do the spinal while you are
out.'

'OK,' I said cautiously. 'I'm in your hands. You are the
doctor.'

Next it was the turn of the orthopaedic surgeon to come,
and suddenly there he was, with his little retinue. Not my
friend the hip and leg surgeon, but the hand specialist! I knew
him to be brilliant at hand surgery, but femurs? He looked like
Rupert Bear, in a bright yellow waistcoat and spotted bow tie.
I smiled wanly.

'I'm the on-call surgeon,' he explained, 'so I will be fixing your leg.'

When he had gone, I asked the nurse if he knew about hips and femurs.

'Oh, I think so,' she said reassuringly. 'I'm sure he's done some.'

As I was trundled to the operating theatre I became very aware of my helplessness as a patient. I was completely in the hands of others. My leg, even my life, depended on their skill. As we arrived at the theatre doors there, to my amazement, was, not just the young anaesthetist, but also the one I had hoped for.

'What are you doing here?' I asked.

'My list has been cancelled, so I thought I would come and lend a hand and join in the fun.' A discussion followed between him and the young doctor about my anaesthetic, and it was agreed to proceed with the ketamine/spinal plan.

I had used ketamine for short-term anaesthetics myself, in Africa. It is used for horses as well as humans. It is safe and easy to administer. But to be at the receiving end of it was something different. I had the most vivid and transcendental experience. I was in a golden room. Everything was bright and shining. Ethereal music was playing. I felt ecstatic. Was I in heaven? No wonder drug addicts abuse ketamine! Then, equally suddenly, I was awake again, my legs numb, my left leg being held aloft by a nurse while it was painted with iodine. The operation began. I felt a sharp sting as the scalpel travelled down most of the length of my thigh.

'Quick! Pass a swab please!' said the surgeon. 'Another! A bigger one! Can you mop please! More swabs!'

'What has he done now?' I thought to myself. 'Does he know where my femoral artery and vein run? After all the leg is not the hand, and he is a hand surgeon.'

The crisis, whatever it was, passed. There was drilling,

and hammering, and screwing. My two anaesthetists and I discussed the current cricket test match.

'That's it. All done,' said the surgeon eventually, stripping off his surgical gloves as he came round to the head end of the table. I noticed that his left hand was heavily bandaged.

'What have you done to yourself?' I asked.

'Oh I just went a bit too far with the scalpel when I made the initial incision,' he said.

All the drama of swabs and blood mopping had been about his blood, not mine.

'Well what a good thing that you are a hand surgeon,' I said.

The post-operative period of recovery and rehabilitation was instructive. I experienced enormous kindness, and also that of, at times, being ignored or avoided, perhaps because I was a doctor. To some staff that fact seemed to be a threat. The most sensitive care came from night staff, who were perhaps not quite so busy with routine duties. The people with time to stop and chat for a few minutes were the cleaners, as they busily redistributed the dust. I tried to be a good patient, not demanding or unreasonable, though at times the pain was so intense that I had to ring my bell. The physiotherapists set me a target, 'Manage these steps with one leg and crutches and you can go home.' I managed in record time. My very own personal physiotherapist, Rosemary, awaited me at home, longing to help me mend and get back to an active life. And so I did, thanks to the skills of paramedics, nurses, a brace of anaesthetists, a brilliant hand-turned-hip surgeon and firm but wonderful physiotherapists—particularly my own. In due course, I was once again able to walk rugged pathways and to climb mountains.

The episode of the fractured leg was for me a sort of Rubicon. I learned acceptance. I accepted that I had passed from the status of doctor to that of patient. I could look back on my professional career with satisfaction and many good memories;

with gratitude for the privilege it had been. Now it was time to put my energies into other things. Not to be 'retired' but 're-tyred', with time for new challenges and opportunities as well as recreation. In the forty-two years since I first qualified as a doctor medicine, and the way it is practised, had changed enormously. Many of the changes have been for the good—computers, mobile phones, clever investigative procedures, amazing surgical techniques, revolutionary new drugs for heart disease, hypertension, diabetes, cancer and so on. So much more can be done both to prevent disease and to treat it. There has been a cost. Of course an enormous financial cost—modern treatments and investigations are hugely expensive. There has also been a cost in the way that medicine is practised. I believe it was a great mistake, in 2004, to release GPs from their 24/7 responsibility for their patients. Out-of-hours doctors and impersonal emergency telephone lines cannot possibly provide the same service that the on-call family doctor once provided. Out-of-hours doctors do not know the patients, and have no access to their medical records. They cover large areas, and cannot possibly make repeated visits during the course of a night, or a weekend.

Consequently they cannot follow up patients, nor provide at-home care for the very ill and the dying. This leads, inevitably, to many unnecessary, and unwelcome, hospital admissions. That, to me, is a very sad loss to family care.

I think of the father of people we know. He was an elderly and frail gentleman, who had come to live out his last days with them. He was not afraid to die. He was tired and ready to go. All he wanted from life was to be surrounded by his family, in their home, and to end his days there. Their own GP knew that. The time for medical interventions had passed. Comfort and quality of life were the priorities. Then one night he became worse and was distressed. The Out-of-hours service was called, and they said that a doctor would visit. In due course he came.

He knew nothing of the medical history. He had no access to medical records. He insisted that admission to hospital was necessary as he would not be able to come back to re-assess the patient. An ambulance was called, and the daughter and son-inlaw followed it to the hospital. When they had parked and found the appropriate ward they were told that the father was 'having tests', and to take a seat. After some time they were told that they might as well go home to bed.

'Can we just see him first?' they asked, and they were grudgingly allowed a brief time with him.

'Now you go home. We will ring you if there is any change.'

On arrival back at home the daughter gave the ward a ring, just to ensure there had been no change since they left the hospital.

'He's fine! Don't you ring us. We'll ring you,' they said. 'Ring in the morning.'

They hadn't long been in bed when the phone rang.

'You'd better come quickly!'

By the time they got to the hospital the father had died. They had been denied their final goodbyes.

To my mind everything that happened that night illustrates the failing, so often nowadays, of end of life care. He didn't need investigations—he had had all those. All he wanted was to have his family around him when he died. All he wanted was to be in their home; for them to be with him, and to hold his hand. Instead he was in a strange department, surrounded by people whom he didn't know, having tests that he didn't need. Why?

Because a highly expensive out-of-hours service could not provide appropriate care.

The time was when his own GP (or at least the partner on call) would have seen him at home, would have had access to his medical records, would have given him treatment to ease his symptoms, and would have called again that night if his condition had worsened. Instead everything happened that he didn't wish, his family were left with unhappy last memories— and a hospital bed was blocked unnecessarily.

Past governments have frequently re-arranged the NHS administrative furniture, each trying to improve efficiency, and to make money go further. Under Mrs Thatcher Fundholding was introduced; then came Clinical Commissioning. Primary Care Groups, Primary Care Trusts, Clinical Commissioning Groups, come and go. Each new Government has a new bright idea, and there is no continuity. No one system is in place long enough for proper evaluation. Whatever future governments may do, in this furniture re-arranging process, my hope and prayer is that general practice, family medicine, will never cease to be a whole life service—with care provided from birth to death; and that it may never cease to be a holistic service— caring for the whole person, body, mind and spirit. It is that which makes it so deeply satisfying and worthwhile. It is that level of satisfaction and fulfilment which makes general practice an attractive career, drawing the best of doctors into this branch of medicine. Why do so few doctors now enter general practice? Why is there such a shortage of GPs? The money is very good, the hours are reasonable, there are no more nights and weekends on call. Is it that red tape has swamped the system? Is there no longer that profound job satisfaction that made it so good to be a GP? Is it that GPs (like teachers) can no longer exercise their professional skills in their own way, but are bound by protocols and procedures?

May we treasure our National Health Service, which, when at its best, is brilliant. May the art of medicine never surrender completely to the science. May person-centred medicine never surrender to disease-centred medicine. There is a wonderful Hebrew word, 'shalom'. It means 'wholeness', 'completeness', 'peace', 'inner harmony and integrity'. In our often dysfunctional and fragmented society the GP is called, not just to treat the disease, but to help each patient, each person, to find 'shalom' in the ups and downs of life. It is to help each patient, each person, to feel valued and cared for. To be the person God intended them to be. That, anyway, should surely be our aspiration and our joy.

ACKNOWLEDGEMENTS

I am grateful to my GP colleagues, with whom it was such a pleasure to work during my thirty years in general practice. We didn't always agree on everything, but we made a strong and loyal team. Also thanks to the entire surgery 'family'—nurses, midwives, health visitors, school nurses, physiotherapists, phlebotomists, receptionists, clerical staff, social workers, cleaners, gardeners and maintenance staff. Everyone contributed to the good reputation of the surgery. We worked hard together—and often laughed together.

Thanks too to our patients, many of whom became friends. Their loyal support of the surgery was always a great encouragement. I am grateful to those patients mentioned in the book whose stories are more recognisable, for their permission to include them. All names of patients have been changed.

I am especially grateful to my wife, Rosemary, and my family, who supported me throughout, and accepted that I could not always be there for them because of work. They too were part of that work, especially during those years when they had to cover the phone for me whenever I was on call. Those were the years when our spouses were, in effect, unpaid, uncomplaining members of the practice.

This book is simply a collection of memories and reflections of a time when general practice was changing quite profoundly. All opinions expressed are entirely my own.

I am grateful to Dr Michael Harper and the Rev'd Dr Mary Barr, and three of my former colleagues, David, Sue and Julian, for checking the script. Also to Katherine Wells for her design of the cover, and to Aspect Design for their efficient help.

All proceeds from the sale of this book will go to the surgery equipment fund, U.M.S.T., hopefully to help provide those extra items which will enhance the standard of care provided. It is gratifying to know that the tradition of excellent care by the surgery lives on.

ALSO BY DAVID WEBSTER

Mishkid—a Kenyan Childhood
The Shimmering Heat—Memories of a Bush Doctor in East Africa.

Both published by Aspect Design, Malvern, Worcester.

Available from the publishers at www.aspect-design.net, Amazon.co.uk or from Dr David Webster, The Grange, Hill End, Upton-on-Severn, WR8 0RN. Email: namirembe@btinternet.com